Great Canadian | 1820 to
Political Cartoons | 1914

BY CHARLES AND CYNTHIA HOU

Moody's Lookout Press

Vancouver, British Columbia

©1997 Charles and Cynthia Hou

Moody's Lookout Press
Vancouver, British Columbia

Canadian Cataloguing in Publication Data

Hou, Charles, 1940-
  Great Canadian political cartoons, 1820 to 1914

Includes bibliographical references and index.
ISBN 0-9680016-1-0

  1. Canada--Politics and government--19th century--Caricatures and cartoons. 2. Editorial cartoons-- Canada--History--19th century. I. Hou, Cynthia, 1941- II. Title.
FC173.H69 1997   320.971'0207   C97-910317-7
F1026.4.H68 1997

Cover design by DesignGeist, based on cartoons by Alonzo Ryan, Owen Staples and J. W. Bengough
Printed and bound in Canada by Hignell Printing Limited

CONTENTS

Preface

"It is often said that a picture is worth a thousand words. A cartoon, well done, is worth a thousand pictures."

John Diefenbaker

Political cartoons provide a graphic view of history in the making. Often exaggerated, and almost always slanted, they both provoke and reflect public interest in the events and concerns of the day.

Unfortunately for the student of Canadian history the best works of our early cartoonists are largely inaccessible. A few collections of historical cartoons have been published, but most are long out-of-print and difficult to find. None gives a truly comprehensive view of our past. *Great Canadian Political Cartoons* fills many of the gaps, resurrecting the works of a number of less well known artists and illustrating more of the significant events and issues in Canadian history.

The cartoons in this collection are drawn from many sources. While most are from Canadian publications, a few relevant British and American cartoons are included. All reflect the attitudes and biases of the individual artists involved and the editorial biases of the publications in which their works appeared. Wherever possible they were selected to present a variety of views of a particular issue. Some of the cartoons relate to isolated incidents, but many events and situations inspired artistic comment over long periods of time. The index provided allows the reader to follow a particular topic or theme over the years.

If Canadian history has one overriding theme, it is the question of survival. Canada's first French Canadian historian, François Xavier Garneau, saw the history of the French in Canada as a continuous struggle. Confronted from the beginning by an inhospitable climate and hostile native people to the south, they later faced the threat of assimilation by the English and domination by the Americans. Many French Canadian cartoons reflect this theme. The attempt of the French to expel the British during the Rebellion of 1837 inspired few if any political cartoons at the time, but the topic appears in a number of cartoons published many decades later. Confederation with the British North American colonies in 1867 provoked a mainly negative response. In the years that followed, French Canadians' attempts to protect their language and religion and to maintain control over their children's education gave rise to a number of cartoons, as did the fear that increasing immigration would further threaten the French culture.

Garneau would probably be surprised to learn how well his ideas would apply to English Canada. English Canadians have feared domination and assimilation by their neighbours to the south ever since the American Revolution of 1775 – 83. At first they clung to the security of their historic ties with Britain, but a Canadian independence movement slowly gained strength. French and English politicians alike argued over the speed at which Canada should assume control over her own affairs. One point of contention was the extent to which Canada should support Britain in the Boer War in South Africa; another was the need to establish an independent Canadian navy. The Alaska boundary dispute of 1903 reinforced the move for independence when Britain, seeking to improve her relations with the United States, sacrificed Canadian interests and gave in to American demands.

Greater independence from Britain brought with it even greater vulnerability to the American threat. At some point almost every Canadian province has had to consider whether or not to join the United States. Border disputes, threats of invasion or annexation, and American cultural influences continued to be frequent topics for cartoonists. Independence also brought greater economic responsibility. Cartoons dealing with Canadian – American trading arrangements and tariffs appear throughout our history.

The aboriginal peoples have waged their own battles for survival. Their way of life was threatened first by French- and English-speaking explorers and fur traders and then by massive immigration and western expansion. The buffalo herds the native people of the prairies relied on for food and other needs were slaughtered, and the people themselves were eventually forced to settle on reservations. Although their problems were generally ignored by mainstream publications, a few cartoons show the difficulty they faced in dealing with a distant and bureaucratic system of government. The Metis sought to maintain their own distinctive way of life in western Canada and often made common cause with the natives. Led by Louis Riel, they confronted Ottawa in 1869 – 70 and again in 1885.

The struggle of the various regions for survival is another recurring theme in Canadian history. The maritime provinces often blame their lack of prosperity on Confederation, and the prairie provinces and British Columbia share many of their concerns. Tariff policies, freight rates, the power of the Canadian Pacific Railway, and federal payments to the provinces are perceived in different ways by each region of Canada, and cartoonists portray the regional discontent.

Many of the cartoons in this book relate to survival on a more personal level, dealing with social issues such as alcoholism and prohibition, disease, drugs, poverty, prostitution, working conditions and political rights for women and minority groups.

Racial prejudice is another well-documented social problem. Western Canada in particular had to absorb large numbers of immigrants in the late 1800s and early 1900s. The Asian immigrants who came to British Columbia at this time bore the brunt of western insecurity. While British and American immigrants were welcomed, Eastern Europeans were seen as a poor second choice and Asian immigrants a distant third. When their labour was needed they were tolerated but when conditions changed they were often the target of vicious racial attacks. Many of the cartoons in this collection present stereotypical views of various groups that are not acceptable today. While we may find them objectionable, they provide an insight into the attitudes that prevailed at the time they were published.

Against the background of recurring themes politicians come and go, and a few play starring roles. Conservative John A. Macdonald led the talks which brought about Confederation in 1867. He became Canada's first prime minister and pursued his dream of a Canada that would stretch from sea to sea. Liberal Wilfrid Laurier, who carried on the work of building the nation, had the ability to deal with the conflicts between English and French that threatened to tear the country apart. Nationalist Henri Bourassa fought to bring about Canadian independence from Britain. Many others have played a significant part in shaping our nation's destiny. None of these figures was faultless, and cartoonists delighted in portraying their flaws. Government in general was a frequent subject and the Senate a ready target.

The cartoons in this collection provide some revealing insights into issues that face Canada today. Many are as relevant now as they were when they were first published. They also provide a richly illustrated view of Canada's past. We hope they will succeed in bringing that past to life and conveying the spirit of our country in its early years.

THE EMIGRANT'S WELCOME TO CANADA

This cartoon, which appeared in the British magazine Punch, *makes fun of poorly prepared emigrants who believed the overly optimistic descriptions of life in Canada published in emigrant guides. It also exaggerates the common British view of conditions in Canada.*

HERE   **AND**   **THERE**

Or, emigration a remedy

Many people saw emigration to the new world as a remedy for overpopulation, unemployment and poverty. This cartoon from Punch *magazine contrasts life for a poor family in the slums of London with a life of plenty in Canada or the United States.*

RIDICULOUS EXHIBITION; OR, YANKEE-NOODLE PUTTING HIS HEAD INTO THE BRITISH LION'S MOUTH.

"WHAT? YOU YOUNG YANKEE-NOODLE, STRIKE YOUR OWN FATHER!"

These cartoons from Punch *refer to the Oregon Boundary dispute, in which Great Britain and the United States both claimed territory located west of the Rockies and between 42 degrees and 54 degrees 40 minutes north latitude. Most of the settlers who had established themselves in the area were American, and the territory was remote. Great Britain therefore agreed to concede the land south of the 49th parallel to the United States. The land to the north is present-day British Columbia. The British cartoonist shows an arrogant "Yankee Noodle" (the United States) confronting the British lion and the symbolic Englishman John Bull.*

THE MAN WOT FIRED THE PARLIAMENT HOUSE!

THE GOVERNMENT THIMBLERIG.

Left. *In 1837 French Canadians failed in an attempt to overthrow British rule. Eleven years later Attorney-General Louis Lafontaine (pictured) introduced into parliament a bill to compensate residents of Lower Canada (Quebec) for the property damage they had suffered. Opposition to the bill led to a riot in which the parliament buildings in Montreal were set on fire.* **Right.** *In 1841 the Act of Union united Upper and Lower Canada. Kingston served as the capital from 1841–1844 and Montreal from 1844–1849. In 1849 the capital was moved once more, to Toronto. Mr. Punch, a character who often appeared in* Punch *magazine, observes the guessing game of thimblerig.*

LITTLE BEN. HOLMES

AND SOME NAUGHTY CHILDREN ATTEMPT TO PAWN THEIR MOTHER'S POCKET-HANDKERCHIEF,
BUT ARE ARRESTED BY POLICEMAN *PUNCH*, WHO WAS STATIONED "ROUND THE CORNER."

THE WAY BROTHER JONATHAN WILL ASTONISH THE NATIVES.

ANNEXATION COMES IN BY THE RAIL, WHILE LIBERTY FLIES OFF IN THE SMOKE.

Left. In 1846 England adopted a policy of free trade. American exports to Britain increased and Canadian exports decreased. The resulting commercial depression led some people to favour the annexation of Canada by the United States. Banker and member of parliament Benjamin Holmes (holding the British flag) actively supported this movement. *Right.* The annexation of Canada by the United States would have seriously threatened French Canadian institutions, laws and language. The majority of Canadians, both English and French, opposed the movement and it quickly collapsed. A sinister-looking Brother Jonathan (top) represents the United States, while the man under the train is French Canadian leader Louis Joseph Papineau.

FUSION DES RACES

EFFET DE LA CONFÉDÉRATION

LE DERNIER COUP DE JOHN BULL.
LES GROSSES MORUES DU GOLFE SONT PRISES.
VIVE LA CONFÉDÉRATION.

Left. FUSION OF THE RACES. *The cartoonist feared that a proposed confederation of the British North American colonies would cause French Canadians to lose their identity. Canada West reformer George Brown (stirring the pot) had long sought to reduce the French influence in Canada.* **Upper right.** THE EFFECT OF CONFEDERATION. **Lower right.** JOHN BULL'S LATEST CATCH. *The big cod of the gulf are taken. Long live Confederation!* [tr.] *Nova Scotia and New Brunswick responded favourably to the idea of Confederation.*

LA CONFEDERATION!!!

Quebec cartoonist Jean-Baptiste Côté portrays Confederation as a many-headed monster and Quebec as a lamb. The figure riding the monster is Upper Canada Reform leader George Brown, and one of the men wafting incense is Lower Canada Conservative leader George Cartier. Both supported a coalition government formed to advance the idea of Confederation.

Signature du Contrat de mariage des deux frères Haut et Bas Canada avec D^{lles} N^{au} Brunswick et N^{lle} Ecosse — Adoption de la jeune île P^{ce} Edouard — La cérémonie se fait strictement en famille, le voisin qui n'a pas été invité n'est pas satisfait — (New-York, Cot. monti à $ 927.03 — Télégr. priv.)

Upper Canada, Lower Canada, Nova Scotia and New Brunswick agree to unite, to the dismay of Uncle Sam, the uninvited guest. Prince Edward Island would join Confederation in 1873.

HOW TO BECOME A CANDIDATE

PERSPECTIVE QUE LA CONFÉDÉRATION
DONNE AUX FAMILLES

LE PASSÉ, LE PRÉSENT ET LE FUTURE DE L'HON. MCGEE

Left. THE EXAMPLE CONFEDERATION SETS FOR FAMILIES. ***Lower right.*** THE PAST, THE PRESENT AND THE FUTURE OF THE HONOURABLE MCGEE. *Thomas D'Arcy McGee, an eloquent advocate of Confederation, was known for his heavy drinking.*

THE QUESTION. CHIEF COOK: *My dear friends, with what kind of sauce would you like to be prepared? Confederation or Annexation?* TURKEYS: *Neither one nor the other!* COOK: *You are avoiding the question!* HUNGRY NEIGHBOUR [Abraham Lincoln]: *I will end up eating both the cooks and the turkey.* [tr.] *An intercolonial railway and representation by population were used to bribe the turkeys (Upper and Lower Canada) to support Confederation. Luther Holton (left) supported annexation by the United States while George Cartier (right) strongly supported Confederation.*

ARRIVÉE DES EMPLOYÉS DU GOVERNEMENT À OTTAWA

ARRIVAL OF THE GOVERNMENT EMPLOYEES IN OTTAWA. Queen Victoria chose Ottawa as the capital of Canada in 1857. Construction of the parliament buildings began in 1859, and they were in use by 1866. The eastern Canadian cartoonist has greatly exaggerated conditions in Ottawa. By the 1860s Ottawa was an important centre connected to the rest of Canada by water and rail networks.

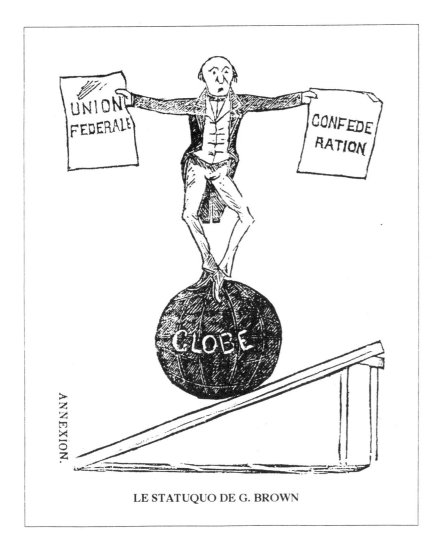

ANNEXION.

LE STATUQUO DE G. BROWN

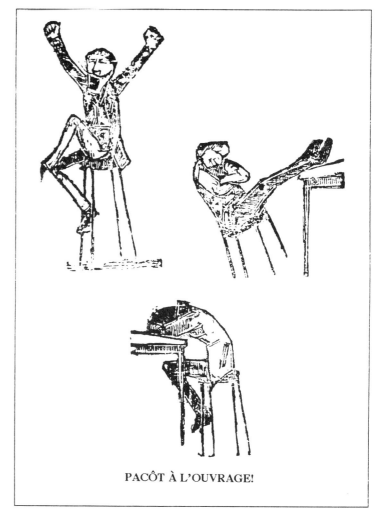

PACÔT À L'OUVRAGE!

Left. GEORGE BROWN'S STATUS QUO. *Reform leader George Brown was editor of the Toronto* Globe. *In 1864 he had played a key role in forming a pro-Confederation coalition government, and he was involved in drafting the terms of union.* **Right.** PACÔT AT WORK. *Cartoonist Jean Baptiste Côté was arrested for publishing these drawings of a civil servant at work.*

During the American Civil War confederate agents sometimes used Canada as a base of operations against the northern states. Now the Fenians, a group of Irish-Americans who wanted to end English rule in Ireland, sought to harm Great Britain by attacking Canada from bases in the United States. The American Brother Jonathan (left) and the British John Bull (right) discuss their common border problems.

"SEWARD'S FOLLY?"
A Purty Big Lump of Ice

In 1867 American secretary of state William Seward (lower left) agreed to purchase Alaska from Russia for $7.2 million. Many Americans felt that their "manifest destiny" was to control the whole of North America. The withdrawal of Russia from North America encouraged American annexationist leaders who hoped to expel Britain from the continent and acquire her remaining possessions. A worried John Bull looks on.

CROSS ROADS
Shall we go to Washington first, or How(e)?

Charles Tupper (left) led the fight to bring Nova Scotia into Confederation in 1867 and continued to work on behalf of Canada. Joseph Howe (in the background) felt that Nova Scotia should remain a British colony, and opposed Confederation until late in 1868. The artist makes it clear that annexation by the United States is a danger to be avoided.

THE ALABAMA CLAIMS

MOTHER BRITANNIA TO MRS. COLUMBIA: Come now – this mess will never get settled, if you allow that boy Jonathan to keep stirring it up.

During the American Civil War, British shipyards sold the Alabama *and several other cruisers to the Confederate states. The cruisers sank many valuable merchant ships belonging to the northern states. After the war the Americans insisted that the British compensate them for the losses, and at one point suggested that British Columbia be ceded to them. John Bull, Mother Britannia (Britain) and Mrs. Columbia (the United States) watch as Brother Jonathan stirs the pot.*

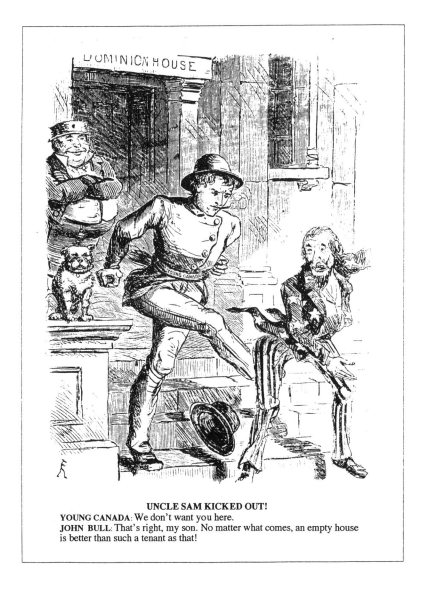

UNCLE SAM KICKED OUT!
YOUNG CANADA: We don't want you here.
JOHN BULL: That's right, my son. No matter what comes, an empty house is better than such a tenant as that!

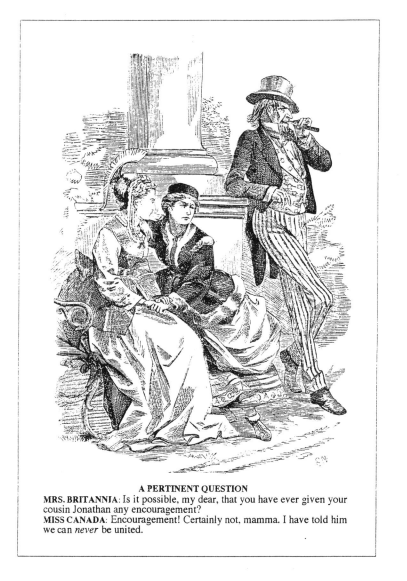

A PERTINENT QUESTION
MRS. BRITANNIA: Is it possible, my dear, that you have ever given your cousin Jonathan any encouragement?
MISS CANADA: Encouragement! Certainly not, mamma. I have told him we can *never* be united.

The possible annexation of Canada by the United States continued to be a matter of concern for Britain as well as for Canada.

FROM HALIFAX TO VANCOUVER

MISS CANADA: This is what we want, cousin Jonathan. It will give us real independence, and stop the foolish talk about annexation. **JONATHAN**: Wal, miss, I guess you're about right thar; but I'll believe it when I see it.

The Americans realized the importance of transcontinental railways in building a strong nation. They completed the Central Pacific and Union Pacific railways across the United States in May 1869 and planned to build another closer to the Canadian border. Such a railway would make it easier to annex all or part of what is now western Canada. This possibility made Canadians realize the need for a transcontinental railway of their own.

THE SITUATION

JOHN BULL KICKING AWAY THE LADDER
He thinks he can do without it, but may find his mistake.

*Left. The woman in the centre of the cartoon represents the Red River colony, which was considering offers of union from both the United States and Canada. **Right**. In the late 1860s some people in Britain began to see the colonies as an unnecessary expense and urged the government to grant them their independence. This cartoon, which appeared in the* Canadian Illustrated News, *suggests that such a move would be a mistake.*

MOTHER BRITANNIA: "CUT HER ADRIFT, EH! HOW DARE YOU?"

Mother Britannia is speaking to British prime minister William Gladstone, whose government favoured a free trade policy and independence for Britain's colonies. Canadian prime minister Sir John A. Macdonald is in the bow of the canoe and George Cartier is in the stern.

CHILD CANADA TAKES HER FIRST STEP
MOTHER BRITANNIA: See! Why, the dear child can stand alone!
UNCLE SAM: Of course he can! Let go of him, Granny; if he falls I'll catch him!

The Americans did not plan to use force to annex Canada. They believed that Canada would sooner or later fall into their hands.

RIEL FOUND OUT!

Metis leader Louis Riel negotiated the entry of Manitoba into Confederation in 1870. A confrontation between Riel and Canadian government surveyor Thomas Scott led to Scott's trial and execution by Riel's provisional government. Riel was held personally responsible by Protestant extremists in Ontario, and was forced to flee Manitoba when Colonel Garnet Wolseley (second from the left) arrived in Red River to restore order.

PROBLEMS FOR THE WISE

A thirsty man, with an empty pocket, opposite a fountain: Result – A hearty drink, a clear head, a healthy stomach, pocket as before.

A tippler, with a shilling and no thirst, opposite a bottle of whiskey: Result – Stupefaction, fever, dyspepsia, and an empty pocket.

Temperance societies were formed in Canada in the 1820s to encourage moderation in the use of alcohol. By the 1850s many groups were calling for its outright ban. The prohibition movement continued to gain popularity in the growing cities, where poverty, ill health and crime were blamed on liquor.

"HUMBLE PIE."

MR. BULL: Humble pie again, William! You gave me that yesterday?
HEAD WAITER: Yes, sir. No, sir. That were Geneva humble pie, sir. This is Berlin humble pie, sir!

Since 1859 England and the United States had disputed the boundary between British and American territory in the San Juan Islands between Vancouver Island and the mainland. In 1872 the German emperor arbitrated the matter and decided in favour of the United States. In another dispute, arbitrated in Geneva, the Americans won a large award for damages done to American merchant ships during the American Civil War.

The march past. — Please drop your eye on the drum-major and the little tootsy-pootsies with the drums.

Life in the camp. — The captain brings her young man round. He feels timid.

WHAT WE MAY (AND OUGHT TOO) SEE IN CAMP SOME OF THESE DAYS

This cartoon may have been inspired by reports from the United States or England, where the struggle for women's rights had already begun.

WHITHER ARE WE DRIFTING?

"WE IN CANADA SEEM TO HAVE LOST ALL IDEA OF JUSTICE, HONOR AND INTEGRITY."—The Mail, 26th September.

Left. *In 1872 members of the Conservative government accepted money from a Montreal businessman who wanted the contract to build the Canadian Pacific Railway. When the Liberals made details of the bribes public, Prime Minister Macdonald attempted to delay the investigation of the Pacific Scandal by proroguing parliament.* **Right.** *Liberal leader Alexander Mackenzie (left) used the Pacific Scandal to help defeat Macdonald.*

THE SCIENCE OF CHEEK; OR, RIEL'S NEXT MOVE.

RIEL (LOQ.)—"FIVE TOUSSAND DOLLARS! BY GAR, I SHALL ARREST ZE SCOUNDREL MYSELF!"

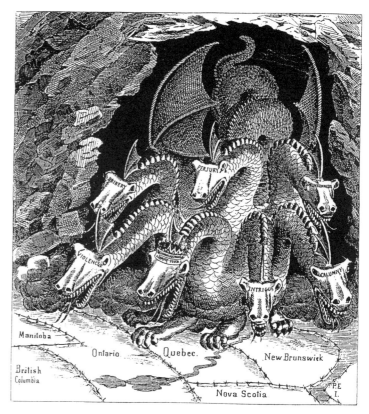

THE ELECTION MONSTER

Left. *Louis Riel was elected in 1873 and again in 1874 to represent Manitoba in parliament, but he was wanted by the Ontario government and could not take his seat. He spent much of the next ten years in exile in the United States.* ***Right.*** *Government corruption was a major theme in the 1874 election.*

LE REMÈDE FUTUR À LA CORRUPTION ÉLECTORALE

ON THE STRIKE

YANKEE PEDLAR: Strike away, boys! Guess I'll take the opportunity to sell Canada all she wants for a year to come; and when you go back to work, I reckon there'll be nothing for you to do!

Left. THE FUTURE REMEDY FOR ELECTORAL CORRUPTION. *The cartoonist suggests imprisonment as a way of dealing with government corruption.*
Right. The American Civil War of 1861 – 65 stimulated the US economy, and American competition posed a growing threat to Canadian businesses. American merchants dumped surplus products on the Canadian market and profited when Canadian workers went on strike.

The terrier is an intelligent and persistent hunter, and the fox is considered to be sly and crafty. In this cartoon Liberal prime minister Alexander Mackenzie is portrayed as a terrier and Conservative Sir John A. Macdonald as a fox. The Pacific Scandal could very well have brought Macdonald's political career to an end; the cartoon suggests that it was too soon to write him off.

BRITISH COLUMBIA IN A PET

UNCLE ALECK: Don't frown so, my dear, you'll have your railway by-and-bye.

MISS B. COLUMBIA: I want it *now*. You promised I should have it, and if I don't, I'll complain to Ma.

In 1871 the Canadian government promised to build a transcontinental railway to link British Columbia to the rest of Canada. Prime Minister Alexander Mackenzie postponed its construction. Influenced by an economic depression and the Pacific Scandal, he decided to build the railway in sections as settlement advanced and public revenues allowed. British Columbia's premier visited first Ottawa and then England to complain about the delay.

PATRIOTISM; AS CONSIDERED BY LEGISLATORS

"To him that hath shall be given,
And he shall have abundance."

"But from him that hath not,
Shall be taken away even that which he hath."

This cartoon contrasts the financial reward given members of parliament with the support given veterans of the War of 1812 and the Rebellion of 1837.

PRODIGE D'ÉQUILIBRE.
Sir John s'exerçant à des tours d'équilibre pour la prochaine session du parlement.

THE POLITICAL BRIAREUS
The versatile candidate making himself all things to all men.

Left. A BALANCING ACT. *Sir John practising his balancing act for the next session of parliament. [tr.] In 1878 the Conservatives won re-election on the strength of a policy designed to boost Canada's depressed economy. The "National Policy" involved the completion of the Canadian Pacific Railway, the settlement of western Canada, and a protective tariff to help Canadian industries compete with American industries.* **Right.** *Like the cartoon on the left, this cartoon illustrates the problems politicians face in meeting conflicting demands.*

JOHNNY AU SUCRE.

Left. SUGAR JOHNNY. *During the 1878 election Sir John A. Macdonald had promoted the idea of a tariff to protect Canadian industries. The cartoonist pictures him at a sugaring operation. As he waits for the maples to flow, his friends in the cabin anticipate the results.* **Right.** *British Columbia member of parliament Amor de Cosmos (left) led the fight in Ottawa to get the long-awaited transcontinental railway built. Prospects improved when Macdonald (right), defeated in his Ontario riding, won a by-election in Victoria. Macdonald's words echo a speech by Iago, a villainous character in Shakespeare's play* Othello.

LA PART DU LION

THE LION'S SHARE. Quebec resented the large amount of money being spent on the extension of the Canadian Pacific Railway to British Columbia. Secretary of State Adolphe Chapleau (centre) stands up for Lower Canada (Quebec) as opposition leader Alexander Mackenzie, Prime Minister Sir John A. Macdonald and Victoria member of parliament Amor de Cosmos look on.

THE HEATHEN CHINEE IN BRITISH COLUMBIA

HEATHEN CHINEE: Why you sendee me offee? AMOR DE COSMOS (The Love of the World or the Lover of Mankind): Because you can't or won't 'assimilate' with us. HEATHEN CHINEE: What is datee? AMOR DE COSMOS: You won't drink whiskey, and talk politics and vote like us.

In the late 1850s and early 1860s many Chinese moved from the California gold fields to the new gold fields in British Columbia. In the 1870s there was both unemployment and considerable anti-Oriental prejudice in British Columbia, and Amor de Cosmos presented a petition to the House of Commons in Ottawa requesting that Chinese labour not be used in railroad construction.

LA PROTECTION

Plus de pain au pays: allons en demander à la terre étrangère.

PROTECTION. No more bread in the country: let's go try somewhere else. [tr.] During the period of economic depression many Canadians were forced to emigrate to the United States to look for work. Although Macdonald's National Policy stimulated economic growth, it did not completely halt the exodus.

LA SEULE CHEMINÉE QUI FUMERA ENCORE APRÈS DEUX ANS DE PROTECTION.

Left. THE ONLY CHIMNEY THAT WILL STILL SMOKE AFTER TWO YEARS OF PROTECTION. *This negative view of Macdonald's tariff policy suggests that it was slow to produce a major improvement in Canada's economy.* **Right.** *Although many immigrants to Canada were poor, some were wealthy themselves and some ("remittance men") were supported by wealthy relatives in England. Their neighbours, who were not as fortunate and had to earn their own livings, often made fun of them.*

He Straightway Secures a Number of Canadian "Souvenir" and "Guide" Books Compiled by Authors With More Imagination than Patriotism.

THE CANADIAN GARGANTUA
This youngster has absorbed the whole of British North America to the wonder of all nations.

In September 1880 Britain transferred the Arctic Islands to Canada, a move which greatly increased the size and prestige of Canada and relieved Britain of an economic burden.

LE PACIFIQUE

BLAKE (montrant la lumière rouge, signal du danger): Arrête, Johnny. Regarde MacKenzie naufragé avec son train. Il n'y a pas encore eu réparations au pont. Tu iras au fond comme Mac.

THE PACIFIC. BLAKE (*showing the red light, a danger signal*): *Stop, Johnny. Look what happened to Mackenzie and his train. The bridge hasn't been repaired yet, and the same thing will happen to you. [tr.] Alexander Mackenzie's slow and cautious approach to railway construction had helped lead to his defeat in 1878. Sir John A. Macdonald was once again prime minister and Liberal Edward Blake was leader of the opposition during the period of major construction of the Canadian Pacific Railway.*

THE SYNDICATE'S CHRISTMAS TREE;

OR, THE TIME FOR GIVING THINGS AWAY.

LE BON SAMARITAIN

Left. The "syndicate" was a group of businessmen who formed the Canadian Pacific Railway Company. Many people resented the special concessions and the enormous grants of land and money made by Prime Minister Macdonald. Liberal leader Edward Blake and Alexander Mackenzie are shown on the left, and Conservatives Sir John A. Macdonald and Sir Charles Tupper on the right. **Right.** Sir Charles Tupper, the new minister of railways, was given the task of building the CPR. He is shown presenting the railway to Miss North West Territories.

LE PACIFIQUE

BLAKE: Tu ne trouves pas ce fardeau trop lourd pour tes épaules? Tu veux te rendre comme cela jusqu'à la Colombie Anglaise!!!
SIR JOHN: Il n'y a rien comme s'habituer à une chose. Regarde un peu. Lorsque j'ai pris ce paquet, il était tellement pesant que jamais je n'ai songé à le porter là-bas. Aujourd'hui je vois qu'il s'allégit à chaque pas que je fais. **BLAKE**: Beau dommage! regarde derrière toi.

THE PACIFIC. BLAKE: Don't you find that burden too heavy? You're going all the way to British Columbia like that!!! SIR JOHN: It's nothing when you get used to it. When I took this pack it was so heavy that I never thought of carrying it that far, but now it's becoming lighter with each step I take. BLAKE: Indeed! Look behind you. [tr.] Liberal opposition leader Edward Blake was a constant critic of the cost involved in building the CPR.

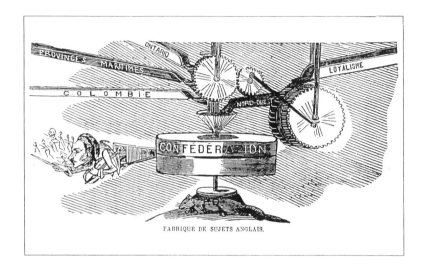

FABRIQUE DE SUJETS ANGLAIS.

BONHEUR DU MATTIN

APRÈS CINQ ANS

Si j'avais pu avoir le courage de rester fille, je n'aurais pas de misère aujourd'hui; et pis dire qu'il y en a tant qui veulent faire c'te folie-là!

LES IMMIGRANTS DU SYNDICAT

Notre agent à Londres nous a fourni la photographie ci-dessus des colons que le syndicat se propose d'établir sur la ligne du Pacifique.

Upper left. THE MAKING OF ENGLISH SUBJECTS. *A Quebec artist compares the process of turning citizens of the English colonies into Canadians to the process used to mill a mixture of grains.* **Lower left.** THE SYNDICATE IMMIGRANTS. *Our agent in London has given us the above picture of the colonists the syndicate proposes to establish along the Pacific line. [tr.]* **Right.** AFTER FIVE YEARS. *If I'd had the courage to stay single I wouldn't have all this misery now; and, sad to say, there are many who want to do the same foolish thing! [tr.]*

LE CALME DE LA VIE CHAMPÊTRE.

———

Ce qui attend le futur colon du Nord-Ouest.

THE *QUIET OF COUNTRY LIFE*: *What awaits the future colony of the North West. [tr.] The French Canadian press was very critical of every aspect of Macdonald's National Policy, including plans to settle the west. This cartoon warns of the hazards settlers might face.*

PARADISE LOST

"And Death grinn'd horrible a ghastly smile to hear
His famine should be filled."   – Milton

ACROSS THE LINE

UNCLE SAM: "National Policy! British Connection! Protective tariff!
Canadian Pacific Railway! Colonization!" And this is your "friendship,"
Sir John! Pshaw!!

Left. John Milton's epic poem Paradise Lost *deals with the struggle between the forces of good and evil, a struggle paralleled in Canadian cities where social problems were a growing concern.* **Right.** *In December 1881 Sir John A. Macdonald announced that the construction of the Canadian Pacific Railway would be completed in five years instead of ten. Uncle Sam (left) realizes that Macdonald's National Policy of railway building, colonization and protective tariffs is designed to thwart his dream of annexing Canada.*

"CENTRALIZATION;" OR "PROVINCIAL AUTONOMY ABOLISHED"
Is this what Sir John is aiming at?

A federal system of government inevitably leads to a struggle for power between the federal and provincial governments. Prime Minister Sir John A. Macdonald wanted Canada to have a strong central government. His frequent disallowance of provincial legislation inspired this cartoon.

FRENCH DOMINATION, PROVINCE D'ONTARIO.

Jean-Baptiste, tel que la peur et l'ignorance le fait voir aux orangistas d'Ontario qui le prennent pour un mangeur d'Anglais.

FRENCH DOMINATION, PROVINCE DE QUEBEC.

Jean-Baptiste, tel que les Anglais pourraient le voir tous les jours, si les préjugés ne les aveuglaient pas, les criailleries des francophobes étant impuissantes à le détourner de la vie paisible et industrieuse qui lui est habituelle.

Left. *FRENCH DOMINATION, PROVINCE OF ONTARIO. Jean-Baptiste, as fear and ignorance make him appear to Ontario Orangemen [militant Protestants], who take him for a monster who would eat the English. [tr.]* **Right.** *FRENCH DOMINATION, PROVINCE OF QUEBEC. Jean-Baptiste, as the English would see him if their prejudices did not blind them, the railings of the Francophobes being powerless to turn him from his peaceful and industrious ways. [tr.] Jean Baptiste personifies a typical French Canadian.*

LE DÉPUTÉ RURAL

Chez lui c'est l'homme le
Plus grand du comté

Mais à Ottawa
C'est un petit homme allez.

THE RURAL MEMBER OF PARLIAMENT. *He's a big man at home, but a little man in Ottawa. [tr.]*

BIRD'S-EYE VIEW OF MANITOBA.

Land speculation was rampant in the west from 1881 until the spring of 1882. Winnipeg, a city of 16 000 people, had 300 real estate agents.

Men outnumbered women in the North West for many years. Emigration societies encouraged unmarried women from England to come to Canada.

THE TOURNAMENT OF TO-DAY.

A SET-TO BETWEEN MONOPOLY AND LABOR.

[FROM *Puck*.

As large-scale industries grew, workers often felt unable to protect themselves from powerful monopolies such as the Canadian Pacific Railway.

THE CHASE AFTER CHANCE

When the government failed to prosecute a group of Masons who conducted an illegal raffle, other groups decided to conduct their own lotteries. The cartoonist suggests that gambling leads only to ruin.

"I STAND FOR JUSTICE; ANSWER, SHALL I HAVE IT?"

THE N. W. T:—I'M GOING TO BE REPRESENTED HERE LIKE MY SISTER PROVINCES, OR KNOW THE REASON WHY!

People living in the North West Territories (present-day Alberta and Saskatchewan) wished to obtain provincial status, which would provide them with local responsible government and parliamentary representation in Ottawa.

GRAND TRIUMPH FOR THE WOMAN SUFFRAGISTS.
MR. MOWAT TAKES THEIR PETITION INTO HIS CONSIDERATION!!

Ontario premier and attorney-general Oliver Mowat was a Liberal known for his cautious approach to politics. In 1883 Ontario women won the right to vote in municipal elections but not in provincial elections. The cartoon suggests Mowat's lack of support for woman suffrage.

THE LEARNED DOCTOR WELCOMING LADIES TO THE PROVINCIAL UNIVERSITY.

In 1884 the Toronto Women's Suffrage Association won women the right to be admitted to the University of Toronto.

WAITING TO SEE WHICH WAY THE CAT WILL JUMP.

In the 1880s public opinion on Canada's future was divided. The "Canada First" group wanted greater independence, some people favoured annexation by the United States, some advocated union with Britain and the other British colonies, and some the unification of all English-speaking people. The three men in the cartoon are Prime Minister Sir John A. Macdonald and Liberal members of parliament Edward Blake and Richard Cartwright.

HIDING FROM THE GREAT UNEMPLOYED.

Fee-fo fi fum,
I fail to hear the N. P. hum.

Where's John A., the man who said
We'd all have plenty work and bread?

The construction of the transcontinental railway failed to attract a flood of settlers to the prairies. Industrial growth was slow and unemployment was high. A group of unemployed workers in Montreal attempted unsuccessfully to meet with Prime Minister Macdonald. Liberal opposition leader Alexander Mackenzie is shown in the distance and Macdonald, author of the National Policy, in the right hand corner.

MASTER OF THE SITUATION

Canadians were reluctant to give the Canadian Pacific Railway yet another subsidy to complete construction. In the cartoon Sir John A. Macdonald (left) and Liberal leader Edward Blake (right) try in vain to drive the CPR hog away from the public trough.

WHAT IT MUST COME TO
(With the Encroachment of Civilization)
OFFICER: [Sir John A. Macdonald]: Here, you copper colored gentlemen, no loafing allowed, you must either work or jump.

This cartoon appeared in a Toronto newspaper on June 20, 1885.

SIR JOHN: (les pieds sur les Métis et le drapeau français): Allons, messieurs les sauvages. Vous êtes rendus au bout de mon territoire. Vous allez sauter dans l'eau du Pacifique ou travailler avec le reste des colons. Choisissez.

SIR JOHN (standing on the Metis and the French flag): Let's go, gentlemen. You have come to the end of my territory. You are going to have to jump into the Pacific or work with the rest of the settlers. Make your choice. [tr.] This cartoon appeared in a Montreal newspaper on July 18.

TOO LATE!

AU NORD-OUEST

Position embarrassée de la justice qui est obligée de s'appuyer sur des baïonnettes pour atteindre Riel.

Left. Sir John A. Macdonald's failure to deal with the grievances of western Canadians led to the outbreak of the Riel Rebellion in late March of 1885. The man in the foreground is Metis leader Louis Riel; the figure in the distance is Macdonald, known as "Old Tomorrow" because of his tendency to put off making decisions. **Right.** IN THE NORTHWEST. The Riel affair puts justice in an awkward position. [tr.] Riel was defeated, arrested, tried and convicted of high treason.

WHAT WILL HE DO WITH HIM?

Prime Minister Macdonald was under conflicting pressure to do nothing and let Riel's death sentence stand, or to recommend mercy.

A RIEL UGLY POSITION.

QUEBEC TO CANADA.

GLORIA VICTIS

A La Memoire

DE

LOUIS RIEL

NÉ À SAINT BONIFACE EN 1844.

MORT À REGINA, LE **16 Novembre 1885.**

Victime du fanatisme orangiste et de son dévouement à la cause de ses frères les métis.

JUSTICE STILL UNSATISFIED

SIR JOHN : Well, madam, Riel is gone; I hope you are quite satisfied.
JUSTICE: Not quite; you have hanged the *effect* of the Rebellion; now I want to find and punish the *cause.*

Facing page, left and upper right. English and French Canadians were divided on the Riel issue. *Facing page, lower right. This cartoon suggests that the rights of the French-speaking Metis were crushed in 1885, just as those of French Canadians had been crushed by the English during the Rebellion of 1837.* **Above.** *To the memory of Louis Riel. Born in St. Boniface in [1844]. Died in Regina, 16 November 1885. Victim of Protestant fanaticism and of devotion to the cause of his Metis brothers. [tr.] Despite all pleas on his behalf, Riel was hung for treason on November 16, 1885.*

THE REAL CHINESE GIANT.

Several thousand Chinese labourers were brought to Canada to help build the Canadian Pacific Railway (the stool is labelled "cheap labour"). As the railway neared completion jobs became scarce, and the workers were encouraged to return to China. To discourage further immigration, Macdonald imposed a head tax of fifty dollars on Chinese entering Canada.

EN ROUTE.

[With Apologies to the Artist of the War News.]

HOW LONG IS THIS SPREE GOING TO LAST?

Left. Canada's large public debt was due mainly to the cost of railway construction. The man on the horse is Prime Minister Sir John A. Macdonald.
Right. Sir John A. Macdonald, shown dancing with Miss Canada, had a well-known drinking problem. The cartoonist compares heavy government spending to a drunken spree.

A GOVERNMENT RESPONSIBLE TO QUEBEC ONLY.

OUR RIGHTS MUST BE RESPECTED AND OUR DEMANDS ACCEDED TO — FOR WE HOLD THE BALANCE OF POWER

(sgd) Quebec

THE WAY THE DOMINION IS RUN.

As Quebec held a large number of seats in the House of Commons, both Liberal leader Edward Blake (left) and Sir John A. Macdonald (right) had to pay close attention to Quebec's concerns. Macdonald's decision to execute Louis Riel was very unpopular in Quebec and there was a shift in support to the Liberal party.

A POLITICAL VIEW OF THE DOMINION SENATE.

The relevance and effectiveness of the Senate is a recurring theme in Canadian history.

WHAT WE RATHER EXPECT.
(Scene – Fishery Commission, Preliminary Session.)

CLEVELAND: Gentlemen, in this business we will have to mutually give and take. Now, let us begin with a clear understanding – I'll take and you give; or, you give and I'll take – just as you like.

In 1887 Canadian representative Sir Charles Tupper (centre) attended negotiations to resolve a fishing dispute with the Americans. Tupper failed in several attempts to link trade concessions with a fisheries agreement. President Cleveland (left) gives Tupper a lesson in American diplomacy while Joseph Chamberlain (right), sent by the British government to negotiate the dispute, watches with amusement. Uncle Sam and John Bull look on.

MISS CANADA, BARMAID
When will the country be "ripe" to get out of this partnership?

PANDORA'S BOX
FINANCE MINISTER MCLELAN: There! Isn't that a grand revenue? And yet these prohibition fanatics would wipe out this remunerative traffic!

These cartoons suggest that the social costs of alcohol abuse exceed the revenues collected by the Canadian government.

PASSING THE BILL
The only way the party leaders will pass it so long as prohibitionists fail to vote as they talk.

THE PROTECTED MANUFACTURER
Bleeding for his country.

Left. *Neither Edward Blake nor Sir John A. Macdonald saw political advantage in championing prohibition.* **Right.** *The cartoonist accuses Macdonald of protecting manufacturing industries which made large contributions to his party at election time. Macdonald's words parody the Latin saying "it is sweet and appropriate to die for one's country."*

JUG-HANDLED PROTECTION

An exhibition of the results of the artificial fattening process in Canada, nine years of experiment.

THE CONSUMER CONSUMED

In the eyes of protectionist statesmanship, the chief function of the consumer is to feed swine.

The protective tariff benefited wealthy manufacturers at the expense of Canadian workers and consumers.

"HOW THE MAP OF THE UNITED STATES WOULD LOOK WITH CANADA ANNEXED"

"CHRISTIAN STATESMANSHIP"

SIR JOHN: Indians starving? Oh, well, they're not "friends of Dewdney," you know. I'll see that *you* don't come to want, though, Mr. Contractor.

Left. One solution to Canada's slow economic growth was commercial union (reciprocity or free trade) with the United States. The Canadian Manufacturers' Association and the Canadian Pacific Railway opposed the scheme, arguing that commercial union would lead to annexation by the United States. The above map, published in an American newspaper, gives credence to this idea. *Right.* Reports of native people starving in the Edmonton area led many to feel that the officials responsible were either neglecting their duties or withholding aid provided by the government. The cartoonist supports the latter view. Edgar Dewdney was lieutenant-governor of the North West Territories at the time.

WHY QUEBEC IS BANKRUPT

"WAITING" FOR TIPS

Left. Quebec prime minister Honoré Mercier (left) was planning to ask Ottawa for aid to reduce the provincial debt of 28 million dollars. The cartoonist blames Quebec's economic problems on the church, which paid no tax on the lands it held and made many demands on government funds. Right. With an election year approaching, both Liberal leader Wilfrid Laurier (left) and Conservative prime minister Macdonald (right) wanted to please Mercier.

THE RIVAL WAITERS (together, and with an earnest desire to please): Anything else you would like, sir? Anything on the *menu*, or anything to order, or anything of any other kind – anything you may wish, or desire, or think of – just mention it, sir, and you can have it!

ANYTHING TO CATCH 'EM!
Casual meeting of two government election workers.

THE DUAL LANGUAGE DUEL

Left. *The cartoonist comments on the duplicity of politicians.* **Right.** *When Manitoba joined Confederation in 1870 the Manitoba Act guaranteed French language rights and the provision of French schools. By 1890 the majority of Manitobans were Anglophone and the government abolished these rights. This action sent a clear message to French Canadians that their rights would no longer be respected outside Quebec.*

TWO OFFICIAL LANGUAGES
"As useless as two tongues on a North-West cart."

The cartoonist supports the concept of one official language for the North West Territories (present-day Alberta and Saskatchewan).

THE GREATEST NATION ON EARTH
UNCLE SAM: We hold that life, liberty, and the pursuit of happiness are the inherent rights of every man! (?)

Canadian nationalists liked to compare the way Americans and Canadians treated their native people. This Canadian cartoon was inspired by the massacre of three hundred native people by the US army at Wounded Knee in 1890.

FRUITS OF THE FRANCHISE ACT

The Dominion election lists are now being revised under an act which discriminates against the poor and industrious, and is in every respect iniquitous and tyrannical, as well as monstrously expensive. Away with it, and *give us manhood suffrage!*

Left. *The issue of the protective tariff dominated the election of 1891. This optimistic view of the benefits to be gained was published by the Industrial League of Canadian Manufacturers.* **Right.** *Until 1918 the right to vote was manipulated by both the Liberal and the Conservative parties. Qualification on the basis of property ownership benefited the Conservative party. The cartoonist supported the concept of "one man, one vote."*

"CAULD KAIL HET AGAIN!"

Bill of Fare for This Session– Soup. Nothing worth mentioning but Soup. The old, pungent, and highly spiced Soup of last session warmed over, but served *ad lib*.

Left. John Abbott (behind the counter) was Conservative prime minister for a year and a half after the death of Sir John A. Macdonald in 1891. **Right.** Abbott delivers the "soup" of a government scandal to Liberals Richard Cartwright and Wilfrid Laurier as Conservative John Thompson watches.

DALY'S MASTERLY INACTIVITY

In the name of justice to the Caughnawagas and mercy to their children, let him hand over the $25,000 due them without further delay.

In 1893 John Thompson replaced John Abbott as Conservative prime minister; Thomas Daly was minister of the interior. This cartoon illustrates the frustrations native people often faced in dealing with government bureaucracy.

WHEN PREMIER LAURIER GOES TO WASHINGTON.

PREMIER LAURIER: Now, it's quite clear that one of us fellows must have control of the other fellow's tariff. The question is, which fellow shall it be?

The cartoonist speculates on the problems Wilfrid Laurier would face if he became prime minister and had to negotiate a trade agreement with the United States without Britain's help.

IRA-T-IL LOIN COMME ÇA?

WILL HE GO FAR LIKE THAT? *In 1890 the government of Manitoba had created a non-denominational school system. This action violated the Manitoba Act and added to deepening divisions between French- and English-speaking Canadians. The Manitoba schools question hopelessly divided the federal Conservative party, which had bases in both Protestant ("Orange") Ontario and Catholic Quebec. Opposition leader Laurier (right) questions Prime Minister Thompson's ability to deal with the issue.*

WILFRID AND THE PORCUPINE.

He has walked all around it several times, but he hasn't really grappled with it yet.

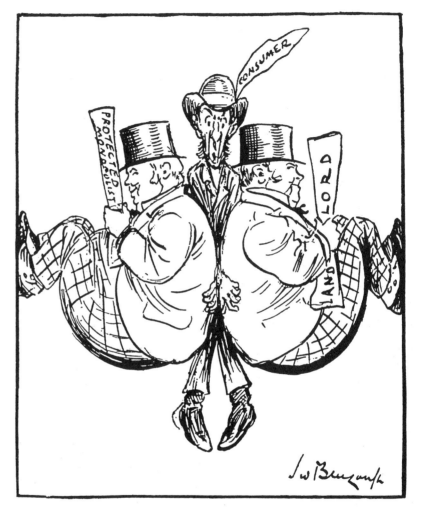

"THE MIDDLEMAN."

Left. Like the Conservative party, the Liberal party was deeply divided on the Manitoba schools question. Laurier was unwilling to deal with the issue. **Right.** The cartoonist supports the view that big business and landlords get more than their fair share of the average consumer's budget.

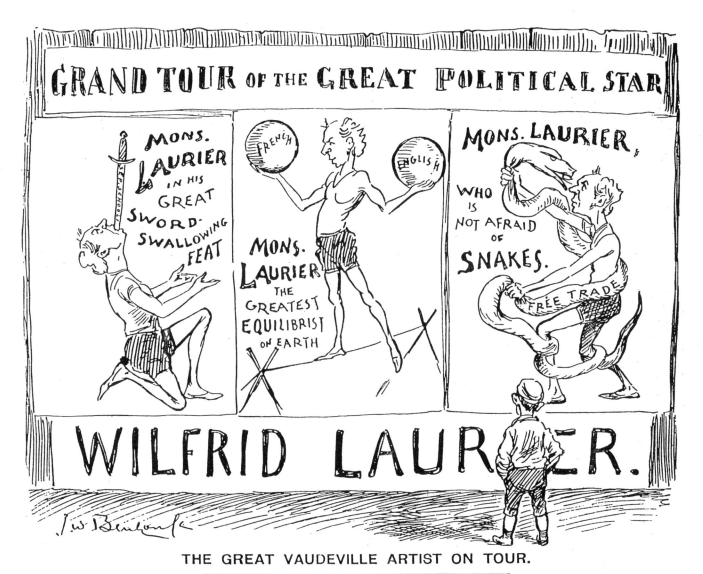

THE GREAT VAUDEVILLE ARTIST ON TOUR.

The cartoonist suggests that Laurier has the ability to balance the interests of English and French Canadians and deal with the problems of free trade.

LA PRESSE HYDRAULIQUE À L'HÔTEL-DE-VILLE

THE BEAR OR THE CUBS

SAME OLD CRY FROM THE BACK GROUND: Why do you confine your efforts to one question? Here are others needing attention. **THE ADVANCED PROHIBITIONIST**: This is the Mother Bear. Help me finish her, and then we'll see about the cubs.

Left. *THE HYDRAULIC PRESS AT CITY HALL. Politicians in 1895 liked to tax and spend just as much as they do today. The taxpayer in this cartoon is being squeezed to enrich the municipal treasury.* **Right.** *Prohibitionists felt that the misuse of alcohol lay behind other social problems. Many favoured giving women the vote as they felt that women would support their cause.*

LA PROTECTION

PROTECTION. *The French Canadian cartoonist proposes a statue to commemorate the regime of Protection in Canada. He obviously believed that finance minister George Foster's protective tariff had failed to guard Canadian interests.*

LA SAISON DU SUCRE

THE CAT CAME BACK
MACKENZIE BOWELL, WILFRID LAURIER, JOE MARTIN: Scat!

Left. SUGARING SEASON. *Wilfrid Laurier (left) was a long-time supporter of free trade, while Conservatives Mackenzie Bowell (standing) and George Foster favoured the protective tariff brought in by Macdonald in 1878. The cartoonist apparently felt that protection was no longer producing benefits and that it was time to try Laurier's policy.* **Right.** *The Manitoba schools question continued to plague politicians. Mackenzie Bowell (upper right) was the new Conservative prime minister, Joseph Martin (lower left) was Manitoba's attorney general, and Wilfrid Laurier (upper left) was the Liberal leader of the oppposition.*

SIR CHARLES TUPPER ET LE PARLEMENT

Ce que les libéraux craignent qu'il ne soit.
Ce que les conservateurs voudraient qu'il fût.
Ce qu'il croit qu'il est.

LES ELEMENTS DU NOUVEAU CABINET

C'est le père Tupper qui va en arracher pour empêcher une FIGHT.

Left. SIR CHARLES TUPPER AND PARLIAMENT. *What the Liberals fear he is. What the Conservatives wish he were. What he believes he is. [tr.]* Prominent Conservative Sir Charles Tupper would soon replace Mackenzie Bowell as prime minister. ***Right.*** THE ELEMENTS OF THE NEW CABINET. *Father Tupper will act to prevent a fight. [tr.]* Sir Charles Tupper's cabinet was badly split over the Manitoba schools question. In 1896 he tried and failed to restore support for separate schools.

ANOTHER ADVENTUROUS INVENTOR.

PERFORMER LAURIER: Yes, my friends, I'm going over in this machine – my own invention – I feel sure it will take me safely through.

'TWIXT AXE AND BOTTLE

UNCLE LAURIER: I'd like a chance to soothe Mrs. Bowell's infant with this bottle.
AUNTY CARTWRIGHT: I'd like a chance to soothe that infant with this axe.

Left. In the 1896 election Laurier moved away from the idea of free trade to a policy of freer trade, reducing but not eliminating tariffs. The cartoonist emphasizes Laurier's lack of principles and predicts his defeat in the coming election. The voters, however, liked his vague policy and elected him with a comfortable majority.   *Right.* Mackenzie Bowell (rear) was now a Conservative senator and Richard Cartwright (right) the minister of trade and commerce in Laurier's Liberal government. Laurier made a few moderate changes to the tariff policy, not the radical changes advocated by Cartwright.

HOW THE NORTHWEST WAS "SETTLED" UNDER THE TORY POLICY

Western Canadians resented the generous land grants and other concessions the government gave the Hudson's Bay Company and the Canadian Pacific Railway, as well as the protective tariff, which effectively raised the cost of supplies.

THE MANITOBA FARMER.

TWIXT CHURCH AND STATE.

Left. *By 1897 an upsurge in world economic activity created growing markets for Canada's agricultural products.* **Right.** *Many people believed in the separation of church and state. The figure to the right of Miss Quebec is Prime Minister Wilfrid Laurier.*

HOW DID HE TAKE IT?

TORY PRESS

GRIT PRESS

ROSYAP.

WILFRID LAURIER:
Oh pretty, pretty, I want that.

JOHN BULL: Wilfrid, you're not going to break Her Majesty's 'art by refusing this 'igh 'onor.

THE MAPLE LEAF FOR EVER!

"HOME, SWEET HOME."

Left. Wilfrid Laurier was granted a knighthood by Queen Victoria during her diamond jubilee in 1897. Although he did not seek the knighthood he liked the political advantages that went with the honour. Right. Sir Wilfrid Laurier returned home in triumph after his trip to England and was welcomed enthusiastically by English and French Canadians alike.

JACK CANUCK "POINTS WITH PRIDE."

UNCLE SAM—Yes, Jack, I'm a pretty considerable big nation, but I see I kin sit at your feet and learn a few things!

Canadians often contrasted the lawlessness of the American frontier with the relatively strict law and order provided by the North West Mounted Police during the Yukon gold rush of 1898.

A PATHETIC APPEAL.

LITTLE CANADIAN PUBLIC OPINION: Father, dear father, come home with me now.

ANOTHER REMOVAL.

VAN (who has taken possession of Parliamentary buildings): Why not? It's where I spend a large part of my time and get in most of my fine work.

Left. This cartoon reflects Conservative fears that Laurier would sell out Canadian interests to the Americans in a free trade agreement. Laurier actually made only modest changes to the protective tariff, lowering tariffs on farm items and on British goods. Duties on American goods would be lowered only if the Americans lowered duties on Canadian goods. The seated figure at the centre is Laurier, and the man behind him is United States president William McKinley. "Father, dear father..." was a popular prohibitionist song of the period. *Right*. Sir William Van Horne was the president of the Canadian Pacific Railway. The CPR prospered along with the rest of the country and had a great deal of influence on the government in Ottawa. In 1898 the federal government gave the CPR a large subsidy to construct a branch line through the Rockies to southeastern British Columbia.

WE WELCOME ALL-THE-WORLD AND HIS WIFE!

Good farms, good homes, good schools and good government for all who will make good citizens.

Clifford Sifton, minister of the interior under Laurier, strongly promoted immigration to Western Canada. He successfully bombarded the United States and Europe with posters, advertisements and pamphlets describing the benefits of settlement on the prairies.

WELCOME TO THE DOUKHOBORS!

JACK CANUCK—Welcome to happy homes in the freest land on earth, and may you all live long and prosper!

In 1899 seven thousand Doukhobors emigrated from Russia to what is now Saskatchewan. They had been persecuted in Russia for refusing to serve in the military, and the Canadian government promised to exempt them from military service.

THE ULTIMATUM.

SIR WILFRID LAURIER: You better let our Bill go through, or you'll feel de weight of this club. See!

COUNCIL OF WOMEN IN SESSION.

Left. Gerrymandering is the drawing of electoral boundaries so as to favour one political party over another. Sir Mackenzie Bowell (right) and other Conservative senators opposed Sir Wilfrid Laurier's attempt to redraw the electoral boundaries set by the Conservatives, and used their power to block the bill. *Right.* The National Council of Women of Canada was founded in 1893. Local councils worked to improve the lives of women and children, seeking such things as better working conditions, the establishment of juvenile courts, and protection for orphaned children. Many of their supporters eventually sought the right to vote so they could more effectively improve conditions in their communities.

SAYS JONATHAN TO JOHN: "It takes two to make a quarrel."

L'IMPÉRIALISME

Malgré les ouvriers et la Colombie Anglaise, Laurier est pour la politique de la "porte ouverte."

Left. *In 1896 gold was discovered in the Yukon. As the shortest route to the goldfields required crossing the Alaska panhandle, Canada claimed the head of some of the fjords to allow miners to reach the Yukon without going through American territory. The Americans claimed that the border was further inland. Britain, which still controlled Canada's foreign policy, was anxious to maintain good relations with the United States.*
Right. IMPERIALISM. *In spite of the workers and British Columbia, Laurier favours the "open door" policy. [tr.] For many years, labour groups and the government of British Columbia had lobbied Ottawa to restrict Chinese immigration to Canada. Mine owners and railway builders favoured Chinese immigrants as a source of cheap, reliable labour, and Laurier was slow to act. In 1900 he would raise the "head tax" on Chinese immigrants from fifty to one hundred dollars. In the same year the Japanese government agreed to restrict emigration of its nationals to Canada.*

Out for Business.

ALL CANADA RALLIES ROUND THE FLAG.
(With apologies to Mr. Kipling.)
But we—we would be true to the Heritage
By more than the word of mouth.

The above poster and cartoon reflect the attitude of English Canadians to the Boer War between the British and the Boers (descendants of Dutch settlers) in South Africa. Many English Canadians enthusiastically volunteered to fight on behalf of Queen Victoria and the British Empire.

"PEACE HATH HER VICTORIES   NO LESS RENOWNED THAN WAR."

Our Honourary Colonel in Peace: Leading the Colonial Contingent in the Jubilee Procession.
[From the Front.]

Our Honourary Colonel in War; Leading the Colonial Contingent in the Transvaal Trouble.
[From the Rear.]

Prime Minister Laurier was placed in a difficult position when Great Britain requested Canadian help in fighting the Boer War. While English Canadians were generally agreeable to the idea, French Canadians were reluctant to participate. The cartoonist contrasts Laurier's display of support for Britain at the 1897 Jubilee celebration in London with his reluctance to involve Canada in the war.

LE SACRIFICE

À l'exemple des femmes indiennes, sir Wilfrid Laurier, pour le succès de son ambition des honneurs et des richesses, va sacrifier son enfant en le jetant dans la gueule du reptile: l'impérialisme. Sir Charles Tupper se porte au secours de l'infortuné. Le sauvera-t-il?

THE SACRIFICE. Following the example of Indian women, Sir Wilfrid Laurier is about to sacrifice his child to the reptile Imperialism to gain fame and fortune. Sir Charles Tupper is coming to the rescue. Will he save it? [tr.] Laurier would eventually send over seven thousand volunteers to South Africa.

THOSE COLONIAL CUBS
Canada scores the first catch.

**THE GREAT CONTINGENT JUGGLER, OR
TRYING TO PLEASE EVERYONE.**

Left. *Canada's first contingent led a brave charge at Paardeburg, which contributed to the first British success in the Boer war.* *Right.* *When Laurier sent the first contingent of one thousand men to South Africa he pledged that he was not setting a precedent for heavier involvement in British imperial wars. A few weeks later he bowed to pressure and authorized a second contingent.*

JOHN BULL: Comme ces Canadiens se souviennent bien, comme ils sont reconnaissants de la tendresse que j'ai témoignée à leurs pères!

400 DE PLUS

Left. JOHN BULL: *How well the Canadiens remember the kindness I showed their fathers!* [tr.] *In 1837 – 38 the British army had brutally suppressed rebellious French Canadians. Now French Canadian volunteers were going to support Britain in the Boer War.* **Right.** 400 MORE. *As the government reserves were almost exhausted, Sir Donald Smith (Lord Strathcona) outfitted several hundred men at his own expense.*

INCERTITUDE

MLLE CANADA: Vous êtes bien aimables, mais je ne me déciderai pas avant l'automne.

UNCERTAINTY. MISS CANADA: You are very kind, but I will not decide before autumn. [tr.] Henri Bourassa (left) was a strong Canadian nationalist. He felt that Canada should be concerned solely with her own affairs and should not become involved in the British imperial struggle in South Africa. Conservative Charles Tupper (far right) favoured all-out support for Britain, while Laurier (centre) favoured more limited involvement.

HIS FAVOURITE PART.

SIR WILFRID LAURIER: You're good friends, boys, and don't want to fight, but for heaven's sake make a bluff and give me a chance to pick up votes on my figger as a peacemaker.

A SHAM.

JOHN BULL---"What Are You So Pleased About, Sam?"
UNCLE SAM---(Chuckling) "Sir Wilfrid Laurier's Preferential Tariff Policy in Your Favour."

Left. The cartoonist suggests that Laurier tended to exaggerate the differences between English and French Canadians in order to enhance his reputation as a peacemaker. In the 1900 election Quebec would vote strongly in favour of Laurier and Ontario would vote strongly Conservative. **Right.** *In 1897 Laurier had brought in a tariff policy intended to favour Great Britain. Although duties against United States goods remained high, American imports rose faster than British imports.*

THE PROFESSOR CONTINUES TO "CUT OFF ITS HEAD
AND TRAMPLE ON ITS BODY" AS PROMISED

BY INDUSTRY HE THRIVES

SIR WILFRID LAURIER: You look as if I'd been makin' you rich.
CANADIAN FARMER: I feel as if I'd been makin' myself rich.

Left. *The elephant symbolized Sir John A. Macdonald's National Policy. When Laurier was in opposition he had criticized Macdonald's protective tariff on imported goods; once elected he did little to change it.*

LIP-LOYALTY VS. LOYALTY THAT ACTS.

Sir Charles Tupper (left) was the leader of the opposition and George Foster (second from left) a fellow Conservative. Liberal prime minister Sir Wilfrid Laurier is on the right. Laurier's preferential tariff for British goods did not impress the Conservative opposition, but it was a big hit in England.

A DANGEROUS BOX TO OPEN.

The cartoonist blames both workers and employers for the problems caused by labour unrest.

L'IMMIGRATION

SIFTON: Voici un joli lot d'immigrants que j'ai eu pour presque rien. MLLE CANADA: Mon Dieu! Combien va-t-il m'en coûter pour les renvoyer?

IMMIGRATION. SIFTON: Here's a fine lot of immigrants that I got for practically nothing. MISS CANADA: My God! How much will it cost me to send them back? [tr.] Between 1897 and 1916 most immigrants to Canada came from the United States and Great Britain. A considerable number, encouraged by Clifford Sifton, came from central and eastern Europe, and a few came from Asia. Many Canadians felt threatened by the influx of foreigners and wondered how Canada could absorb them all. The cartoonist has drawn exaggerated stereotypes of the immigrants to show his disapproval.

PROTECTION CONTRE L'IMMIGRATION

BAPTISTE: Laurier, ces gueux-là vont me voler mon dîner! LAURIER: Aie pas peur, Baptiste! Je te protège contre les Américains.

PROTECTION AGAINST IMMIGRATION. BAPTISTE: Laurier, those rogues want to rob me of my dinner! LAURIER: Don't be afraid, Baptiste! I'll protect you from the Americans. [tr.] The cartoonist portrays the threat that overseas immigrants posed to workers in Quebec. An oblivious Laurier defends Baptiste against the empty threat posed by American workers.

APRÉS LE RECENSEMENT
BAPTISTE: Attend encore dix ans, mon petit John Bull, et tu n'en mèneras pas large.

AFTER THE CENSUS. BAPTISTE: Wait ten more years, my little John Bull, and you will be in a tight corner. [tr.] The 1901 census showed rapid growth in the French-speaking population of Quebec. This growth would soon be offset by an immigration policy that encouraged large numbers of English-speaking settlers and settlers who would adopt English as a second language.

JEAN BAPTISTE N'EST PAS IMPÉRIALISTE
LE BRITISHER: Ainsi vous n'êtes pas impérialiste. JEAN-BAPTISTE: Paraîtrait que non.

JEAN BAPTISTE IS NOT AN IMPERIALIST. THE BRITISHER: So you are not an imperialist. JEAN-BAPTISTE: It would appear not. [tr.] Jean Baptiste recalls the execution of French Canadians after the Rebellion of 1837 – 38.

NATIONAL SPORT.

He can be beaten at yachting, rowing, running, bicycling and every other sport, but holds the world's championship at his favourite amusement.

L'IMPÉRIALISME À LA TUPPER
De cet impérialisme, le Canada n'en veut pas.

*Left. A Canadian view of America's racial problems. **Right.** IMPERIALISM À LA TUPPER. Canada doesn't want any of this imperialism. [tr.] The figure on the right is Joseph Chamberlain, British secretary of state for the colonies. Chamberlain promoted the idea that the British colonies should unite in an imperial federation, contribute to an imperial army and navy, and agree to a commercial union. Despite the obvious threat to Canadian autonomy and tariff protection, Conservative Charles Tupper was receptive to the proposal. The cartoonist portrays him licking Chamberlain's boots.*

LE CHEVALIER ET LE DRAPEAU

LAURIER : L'important c'est de rester en bons termes avec la belle. Je me montrerai quand le combat sera fini.

THE HORSEMAN AND THE FLAG. LAURIER [in the background]: The important thing is to stay on good terms with the beautiful maiden. I will show myself when the fight is over. [tr.] Laurier personally believed that Canada should not have become involved in the Boer War. He was not unhappy when Henri Bourassa led a group of young French Canadian nationalists in a campaign against imperialism.

LA PROHIBITION – ONTARIO ET QUEBEC
QUÉBEC: À ta santé Baptiste.

MRS. BROWN RETURNS FROM THE WCTU CONVENTION
A DAY EARLIER THAN MR. BROWN EXPECTED.

Left. PROHIBITION – ONTARIO AND QUEBEC. QUEBEC: *To your health, Baptiste. [tr.] The prohibition movement was gaining strength in Ontario, though not in Quebec.* **Right.** *The Women's Christian Temperance Union led the fight for prohibition.*

Left. Laurier and British colonial secretary Joseph Chamberlain discussed Canadian–British affairs at a conference on imperial unity. Laurier was prepared to consider ways of improving trade within the empire, but opposed proposals that Canada contribute to imperial defence.

THE "LITTLE CANADA" PARTY: What? – We get off and help him up the hill? – Why, the idea!

L'IMPÉRIALISME AMERICAIN
Encore un pas et...

THE AMERICAN EAGLE: Let me see; what else is in sight now?

Left. AMERICAN IMPERIALISM. *Another step, and ... [tr.] In 1898 the US went to war with Spain. The Americans won the war and took possession of Puerto Rico, Guam, the Philippines and Cuba. They annexed the Hawaiian Islands the same year. Could Canada be next?* **Right.** *The island of St. Pierre (the rooster) is a French colony off the coast of Newfoundland.*

THE GROWING TIME FOR TRANS-CONTINENTAL RAILWAYS

THE PREMIER: The people pay for and give you the Railways, and make you a present of the country: but what do they get as a *quid pro quo*?
CHORUS: The people, as represented by the government – will get – er – our vote and influence, you know.

Encouraged by a period of economic expansion, Laurier decided to enlarge Canada's rail network. The cartoonist exaggerates the number of railways to be built and anticipates the usual heavy government subsidies.

A HARD HAND TO BEAT

WHAT CANADA SHOULD DO

UNCLE SAM: All I'm scared of is that Johnny Canuck may put the export duty stop-log in, cut off my supply of logs and then turn the water into the natural channel leading to his own mills.

Left. *The worker feels that powerful employers hold all the best cards, controlling the courts, the militia, the government and the police.* *Right.* *By the end of the nineteenth century pulpwood was in high demand. Many Canadians favoured an end to the export of raw logs and the development of a pulp and paper industry. A heavy duty on exported logs would encourage such development.*

SOME OF THE STRANGE GODS WORSHIPPED IN JOHNNY CANUCK'S TEMPLE OF FAME.

Canadians often tend to look elsewhere for advice and expertise.

THE MAN WITH THE ELEPHANT ON HIS HANDS

Minister of the Interior Clifford Sifton encouraged the Doukhobors to immigrate from Eastern Europe. The Doukhobors rejected secular government. They did not like to register land under individual names; to register all marriages, births and deaths; or to send their children to school. The Russian in the background is apparently amused by the trouble they were causing Sifton.

GERMANS   ICELANDERS   SCOTCHMEN   ENGLISHMEN   AMERICANS   FRENCHMEN   SCANDINAVIANS

BELGIANS   RUSSIANS   AUSTRIANS   IRISHMEN

THE MAPLE LEAF   FOR EVER

"NOW THEN, ALL TOGETHER"!

One of a number of illustrations published by Minister of the Interior Clifford Sifton to promote immigration to Canada.

LE RETOUR DE BAPTISTE

BAPTISTE: Adieu l'oncle Sam, je retourne au Canada, sous le gouvernement Laurier la prospérité est revenue au pays.

LE CANADA POUR LES CANADIENS

BAPTISTE: Bien sûr que je vais me donner une indigestion, si je mange tout cela seul; je ferais peut-être mieux d'inviter mes voisins.

Left. BAPTISTE'S RETURN. BAPTISTE: *So long, Uncle Sam, I'm going back to Canada. Under Laurier's government, prosperity has returned to the country. [tr.] In the late 1800s many people from Quebec left Canada to work in the United States. By the early 1900s Canada's forest products and minerals were in demand and railway development opened up settlement possibilities in northern Quebec. Many of those who had left returned home.*
Right. CANADA FOR CANADIANS. BAPTISTE: *I'm going to get indigestion for sure if I eat all that myself; perhaps I'd better invite my neighbours. [tr.]*

THE NEW BELLE

MISS COLUMBIA: She certainly is attracting a great deal of attention, and though I'm sorry they're leaving me, I do admire my fair cousin.

Once the best agricultural land in the United States was taken, emigration from Europe and the eastern United States was diverted to western Canada. Suddenly Miss Canada found herself the centre of attention. Miss Columbia (representing the United States) looks on.

A FINE DISTINCTION

SIR WILFRID: Treat you the same way, Mr. Jap? By no means! I haven't the remotest intention – not while you have that club!

The Canadian government increased the discriminatory head tax on Chinese immigrants from fifty dollars to one hundred dollars in 1900 and five hundred dollars in 1903. While China was a relatively weak power, Japan had a strong army and navy and had formed an alliance with Great Britain to check Russian expansion in Asia. Canada had no wish to jeopardize her own or Britain's relations with Japan.

**A LITTLE GAME OF "CONCESSION" POKER NOW
GOING ON IN LONDON – FIND THE WINNER**

LA FRONTIÈRE DE L'ALASKA

Left. In 1903 the long-standing dispute over the Alaska–Canada border was sent to an arbitration tribunal. Canadian foreign affairs were still handled by the British Foreign Office. **Right.** THE ALASKA FRONTIER. Canadians were concerned about negotiations on the location of the border.

HOW CANADA IS ALWAYS SERVED.

WAITER ALVERSTONE (of the Fat-head Diplomacy Cafe): 'Oping you'll pardon, sir, the mutilation of your order, sir. I took the liberty of cutting hoff a wing for that colonial feller that's just gone hout.

The commission appointed to deal with the Alaska boundary dispute had six members: two experienced judges from Canada, one from Britain and three political appointees from the United States. British representative Lord Richard Alverstone voted against the Canadian claims. The award gave the United States a wide enough panhandle to cut off all water access to adjacent Canadian territory.

THE CANADIAN COMMISSION STARTS HOMEWARD.

THE BEAVER: You fellows can purr and screech all you like over the result, but I'm going home to dam.

LE POUVOIR DE TRAITER

LAURIER: Passez-moi cette massue, John, et s'il nous arrive encore des accidents, nous n'aurons que nous à blâmer!

Right. TREATY-MAKING POWER. *LAURIER: Hand over that club, John, and if we have any more problems we'll have only ourselves to blame! [tr.]*
Canada walked away from the Alaska boundary affair determined to gain greater control over its external affairs.

IF CANADA HAD TREATY-MAKING POWERS INDEPENDENT OF GREAT BRITAIN'S AID

The cartoonist suggests that Canada should not be in too great a hurry to gain full control over its foreign affairs.

JOHN BULL: Yes, 'e's makin' a lot of noise, Sam, but 'e'll get over it.

Although the Americans had a strong case in the Alaska boundary dispute, Canadians were upset with their lack of fair play and with Britain's willingness to give in to their demands. Bourassa cited this "stab in the back" as evidence that Canada could never count on the British foreign office. This cartoon presents an American view of the dispute.

LES BEAUTÉS DE L'IMPÉRIALISME
JOHN BULL: Aidez-moi donc! CANADA: Jamais de la vie.

ANNEXION
BAPTISTE-CANADIEN: Certainement, que je suis en faveur de l'annexion!

Left. THE BEAUTY OF IMPERIALISM. JOHN BULL: Give me a hand! CANADA: Not on your life. [tr.] Canada enjoyed the benefits of imperial defence without the associated costs. Right. ANNEXATION. BAPTISTE. Certainly, I'm in favour of annexation! [tr.] This cartoon and the one opposite illustrate the confidence Canadians felt during years of unprecedented growth.

LE MOMENT PSYCHOLOGIQUE
LE CANADA: Me voilà homme maintenant et il me faut un habit neuf.
Lequel vais-je choisir. Celui de l'impérialisme est trop large et pas assez
long; celui de l'annexion est trop long et pas assez large. Je crois qu'une
bonne tuque et un capot d'étoffe, sont encore ce qui m'irait le mieux.

Notre Drapeau National

Left. THE MOMENT OF DECISION. CANADA : *Now that I'm a man I need new clothes, but what shall I choose? The imperialism outfit is too big and not long enough, and the annexation outfit is too long and not big enough. I think a good tuque and a cloth coat still suit me best. [tr.]* **Right.** OUR NATIONAL FLAG. *The strongest movement for a distinctive Canadian flag came from Quebec. The design of this early proposal, combining the French tricolour and the maple leaf, closely resembles the flag adopted by Canada in 1965.*

LA VRAIE VICTIME DES GRÈVES, C'EST LE PUBLIC.

LA QUESTION OUVRIÈRE
Il ne faut pas se fier aux apparences.

Left. *THE PUBLIC IS THE TRUE VICTIM OF THE STRIKES.* **Right.** *THE LABOUR QUESTION. One should not trust appearances. [tr.] Between 1901 and 1911 there were over a thousand labour disputes in Canada as workers sought union recognition and higher wages.*

WRECKERS OF INDUSTRY
Three striking features of alien labor agitators.

WHY NOT HAVE ANOTHER STRIKE?

*Left. Many Canadian workers joined American unions, and business interests blamed industrial unrest on alien labour agitators. **Right.** The cartoonist suggests that housewives should employ the strike tactic to improve their own working conditions.*

HE DID IT WITH HIS LITTLE CONGRESS.

UNCLE SAM: Say, whenever I look at that plugged-up tunnel an' that thar di-verted stream, waal, I jest wanter sit up nights an' kick myself.

THE TIMID CANADIAN SEES A TERRIBLE APPARITION.

Left. In 1866 the United States had allowed its 1854 reciprocity treaty with Canada (the Abrogation Treaty) to expire. As American western expansion slowed down and Canadian expansion accelerated, the US became more interested in trade with Canada. **Right.** Opponents of free trade with the United States are accused of raising unjustified fears of Americanization.

JONATHAN: Baptiste croit faire de bonnes affaires; ce que je vais me payer sa tête quand je lui aurai chippé tout son bois.

OUT FOR AN UN-"CONSTITUTIONAL"

How far does the cow-boy President intend going?

Left. JONATHAN: *Baptiste thinks he has gotten a good deal, but I'm playing him for a fool by taking all his wood. [tr.] A Quebec cartoonist urges Canadians to build a pulp and paper industry in Canada instead of exporting raw logs to the United States.* **Right.** *After US president Theodore Roosevelt's success in the Alaska boundary dispute, he sought control of the Panama Canal zone.*

AUCTIONEER JOHNNY CANUCK: "Now, Gentlemen, make your bids. How much am I offered?"

Starting in 1897, Canada offered to reduce its tariffs for any country that would offer Canada similar lower rates.

LE "GERRYMANDER"

Sir Wilfrid, le chevalier sans peur des temps modernes, vient d'effacer, d'un coup de rapière, le triste chef-d'oeuvre de Sir John A. Macdonald.

DE MONCTON À WINNIPEG

Un grand pas dans la voie du progrès vient d'être fait par Sir Wilfrid Laurier.

Left. THE "GERRYMANDER." *Sir Wilfrid, the fearless modern day knight, has just slain Sir John A. Macdonald's sorry masterpiece. [tr.] Macdonald's government had "gerrymandered" the electoral boundaries to favour the Conservative party. In 1903 the Liberals finally succeeded in redrawing the boundaries.* **Right.** FROM MONCTON TO WINNIPEG. *Sir Wilfrid Laurier has just taken a great step forward. [tr.] In 1903 Laurier named Moncton as the eastern terminus of the National Transcontinental Railway. Laurier sanctioned two new railways from coast to coast as part of his plan to service the needs of the new settlers. The figure in the foreground is Andrew Blair, the minister of railways and canals.*

NOUVEAU TRANSCONTINENTAL

BAPTISTE: Oui, c'est certainement une bonne chose, mais puisque nous devons le payer, il devrait nous appartenir.

LES DIVERSES OCCUPATIONS DE NOTRE PREMIER MINISTRE

Left. NEW TRANSCONTINENTAL. *BAPTISTE [to Laurier]: Yes, it's certainly a good thing, but since we have to pay for it, it should belong to us. [tr.] Laurier's plan to expand Canada's railways was popular from coast to coast. The government paid for and owned the National Transcontinental Railway and gave financial aid to the Grand Trunk Pacific Railway.* **Right.** *THE DIVERSE OCCUPATIONS OF OUR PRIME MINISTER.*

LES ENLÈVEMENTS

Pauvres petits imprudents, vous devriez demander un arbitrage.

ORPHÉE

On n'a attrape pas les mouches avec du vinaigre.

Left. THE KIDNAPPINGS. *Poor little fools, you should ask for arbitration. [tr.] The United States acquired Cuba, Puerto Rico, and Hawaii in 1898; in 1903 it received a favourable arbitration award in its border dispute with Canada over Alaska, and acquired rights to the Panama Canal Zone.*
Right. ORPHEUS. *One doesn't catch flies with vinegar. [tr.] Sir Wilfrid Laurier is portrayed as Orpheus, a figure in Greek mythology whose music could charm wild animals. The cartoon anticipates that Canada will follow the American lead and expand to include Greenland, Labrador, Newfoundland and the islands of St. Pierre and Miquelon. Unlike Uncle Sam, Laurier is not planning to use force.*

LE CANDIDAT ET L'OUVRIER.

Avant.   Après.

HE PROMISED TO FOLLOW IT.

DR. NESBITT: I agree with Mark Twain – "Be good and you will be alone."

Left. THE CANDIDATE AND THE WORKER. Before and after. [tr.] **Right.** *Not everyone favoured the prohibition of alcohol. A majority of Canadians likely agreed with American author Mark Twain and William Nesbitt (right), a Conservative in the Ontario legislative assembly.*

PAS DE "PORTE OUVERT" AU CANADA

"ANGLO-SAXON TORONTO"

Left. NO OPEN DOOR IN CANADA. *In 1903 Prime Minister Laurier had raised the head tax on Chinese immigrants to five hundred dollars.* **Right**. *Many immigrants to Canada settled in Toronto and Montreal. The cartoonist disputes a public speaker's comment that Toronto was "the most thoroughly Anglo-Saxon city in America."*

Although Canada had many attractive features, the availability of vacant land in the west likely played the most important role in attracting immigrants from the United States.

GO WEST YOUNG MEN

BAPTISTE: Voyez donc avec quel empressement John Bull et l'Oncle Sam pénètrent dans le Nord-Ouest. Mon Dieu! Si je ne me dépêche pas, il n'y aura bientôt plus un pouce de terre pour le Canayen.

LE RÊVE DE BOURASSA
Le réveil a été cruel.

Left. GO WEST YOUNG MEN. BAPTISTE: Look at John Bull and Uncle Sam heading for the North West! If I don't hurry, there won't be any land left for me. [tr.] Roughly seventy-five percent of immigrants to Canada came from Great Britain and the United States. Right. BOURASSA'S DREAM: The awakening was cruel. [tr.] The man on horseback is Quebec member of parliament Henri Bourassa, and the men impaled on his lance are British colonial secretary Joseph Chamberlain, John Bull and Uncle Sam. Although Bourassa was considered a traitor by many English-speaking Canadians at the time, his strongly nationalistic ideas were eventually accepted by most Canadians.

BETRAYED AND THROWN
SIR WILFRID: Ah! My dear Sifton, you've thrown him down beautifully.

A crisis arose in Ottawa when the new provinces of Alberta and Saskatchewan were created in 1905. Laurier favoured a system of separate and equal Catholic and Protestant schools. Many western Canadians opposed the idea. Although the cartoon suggests otherwise, Minister of the Interior Clifford Sifton was among them. He resigned from Laurier's cabinet over the issue.

A SQUARE PEG IN A ROUND HOLE
SIR WILFRID LAURIER: It shall go in in spite of the damage done.

QUESTION DES ÉCOLES

Left. Laurier was initially unwilling to modify his separate schools proposal but was eventually forced to do so. *Right.* SCHOOLS QUESTION. Laurier's party was reunited by his changes to the separate schools proposal, but militant Protestants (Orangemen), the Catholic church and nationalist Henri Bourassa remained angry with the compromise.

SIR WILFRID: I don't think these cutlets are good for you, my dear Alberta, so I'll just eat 'em myself. But you can ask a blessing, if you like.

When Alberta and Saskatchewan became provinces in 1905 the federal government retained control over their natural resources. Frank Oliver (left) was a member of parliament for Alberta. He was made minister of the interior by Sir Wilfrid Laurier (centre) when Clifford Sifton resigned.

SHARING THE BURDEN

JOHN BULL (quite upset, as his friend gives him an unexpected lift): Eh!
What! Oh, I say, this is so sudden!

SUPPRIMONS LE VICE
La police de Montréal écrasant la tête du serpent Chinois.

*Left. When Britain decided to close its naval bases at Esquimalt in the west and Halifax in the east, Canada took them over. **Right.** DOWN WITH VICE. The Montreal police crushing the head of the Chinese serpent. [tr.] Opium use was legal in Canada until 1908, when the trade was driven underground.*

In a speech in the British Columbia legislature, Premier Richard McBride complained that British Columbia contributed more to Canada financially than it received in return. The house passed a resolution calling for better terms. This cartoon was drawn by BC artist Emily Carr.

BAPTISTE ET L'IMMIGRATION

CES PAUVRES PERSÉCUTÉS

Left. BAPTISTE AND IMMIGRATION. *Baptiste urges Minister of the Interior Frank Oliver to recruit immigrants from Quebec rather than to empty the prisons of Europe.* *Right.* THE PERSECUTED. *The Jew and the Oriental share their feelings of persecution as Baptiste attempts to drive them away.*

L'ENFANT PRODIGE

THE CHILD PRODIGY. The growing popularity of Henri Bourassa's campaign for Canadian independence worried both Sir Wilfrid Laurier (left) and Conservative leader Robert Borden. Laurier wanted to maintain at least some ties with Britain, and Borden wanted an even stronger British connection.

L'INDEPENDANCE !

L'Angleterre semble vouloir en prendre à son aise avec "nos droits" – les "États-Unis" semblent tout disposés à les accepter ces mêmes droits. – Mais il y a le glaive de l'Indépendance, y a ça, voyez-vous!!!!

INDEPENDENCE! *England seems ready to hand over our rights, and the United States seems ready to accept them. But watch out for the double-edged sword of independence! [tr.] Many French Canadians saw themselves as the defenders of Canadian independence. Bourassa dreamed of a Canada where both founding races would have equal rights, and opposed interference by Britain and the United States.*

IF RENTS GO MUCH HIGHER

The population surge in many cities drove up real estate prices and the cost of rental accommodation. Some people were forced to live in tents.

NOTRE IMMIGRATION!

CB: Wilfrid, protège-moi contre ces maudites bêtes!

"A TALE OF TWO CITIES."

Left. OUR IMMIGRATION! BRITISH COLUMBIA: Wilfrid, protect me from these damned beasts! [tr.] An Anglo-Japanese treaty signed in the summer of 1907 led Japan to abandon its voluntary emigration restrictions. Changes in policy resulted in a surge of immigration from Japan to British Columbia. **Right.** On September 7, 1907, an anti-Asiatic parade in Vancouver ended in a riot and an attack on the Chinese and Japanese sections of the city. This cartoon appeared in an American newspaper.

HAND PICKED ONLY
JACK CANUCK: I want settlers, but will accept no culls.

THE SAME ACT WHICH EXCLUDES ORIENTALS SHOULD OPEN WIDE THE PORTALS OF BRITISH COLUMBIA TO WHITE IMMIGRATION.

Many Canadians called for a more selective immigration policy favouring the more readily assimilated white immigrants over Asians.

HAPPY THOUGHT!
(Rudyard to the Rescue.)
"I have it! Listen, now. Cram the country full of your own kinspeople, and there simply won't be room for the Asiatics!"

Imperialistic British author Rudyard Kipling visited British Columbia in 1907. His views reflected the opinion of most British Columbians at the time.

HINDOO BRITISH SUBJECT: Alas! I must be mistaken! I thought the word "British" meant Freedom and Liberty!

LOOKING AHEAD
What it may come to if the oriental invasion is not stopped.

Left. In January 1908 the federal government decided to restrict Oriental immigration by requiring immigrants to come directly from their countries of origin by a continuous passage. As a direct steamship route from India to Canada did not exist, this measure effectively stopped immigration from India. *Right.* Many British Columbians dreaded an "oriental invasion." The continuous passage bill, the renewal of Japan's voluntary emigration restrictions, and the head tax on Chinese immigrants would eventually allay their fears.

AS THE SNOW OF CONCEALMENT DISAPPEARS
HEAD OF THE HOUSE [Laurier]: This is a job I allus hate.

AU CONSEIL DE VILLE
L'ENTREPRENEUR ANGLAIS: Toi, Baptiste, tu peux lui têter la queue.

Left. Government involvement in economic development and political patronage resulted in charges of corruption in the 1908 election.　**Right.** AT CITY COUNCIL. ENGLISH ENTREPRENEUR: You, Baptiste, can milk the tail. [tr.] Resentment was growing over English domination of the Quebec economy.

IF

R.L. BORDEN, MP: I'd be taller than you if I had French Heels.

HIS OLD MAN OF THE SEA

JACK CANUCK: It wouldn't be so bad if he'd only drop a few of his sticks and crutches.

Left. Thanks to his strength in Quebec, Prime Minister Laurier (left) defeated Conservative leader Robert Borden in the 1904 and 1908 elections. *Right.* Members of the Senate were appointed for life by the prime minister.

A DANGEROUS LEVEL CROSSING.

The Senate is portrayed as an anachronistic body out of touch with public opinion.

AN IMPORTANT CONFERENCE

American president Theodore Roosevelt was a strong environmentalist. This American cartoon shows Uncle Sam inviting Canada and Mexico to join him in a plan to preserve North American forests. The size of the forest suggests that his proposal may have come too late.

THE DOOR STEADILY OPENS

The Grain Grower's Guide, *a prairie newspaper, was an early supporter of women's rights. This cartoon suggests that once women get the vote they will eliminate such vices as alcoholism, gambling, white slavery (prostitution), corruption and graft.*

MRS. PANKHURST, at Toronto: The day will come when women will sit in your Canadian Parliament. (Cheers).

DANGEROUS
Watch us crowd the big fellows.

Left. Emmeline Pankhurst was a British feminist who visited Canada in 1910. **Right.** Canada did not have a navy and was dependent on Britain for her coastal defence and the defence of her merchant fleet. Germany was now challenging Britain's naval supremacy, and Canadians felt that Canada should contribute financially to the British fleet. Prime Minister Laurier proposed that Canada should build her own navy, termed the "tin-pot navy" by Conservative critics of the idea.

TRYING TO SPLIT THE NATIONAL TREE

LA QUESTION BILINGUE DANS ONTARIO

LE PAPA CANAYEN: Si c'est une bataille à coup de poings qu' tu veux maudit "arrangiste," j'vas te donner ça dret, fret, net sec. Tu n'as qu'à te planter pour le premier et je te fourrerai le s'cond.

Left. Quebec nationalist Henri Bourassa accused Prime Minister Laurier of ignoring the right of French Canadians to maintain their own language and culture outside Quebec. The Ontario cartoonist accuses Bourassa of driving a wedge between French and English Canadians. **Right. THE BILINGUAL QUESTION IN ONTARIO. PAPA CANADA:** *If it's a fist fight you want, you damned Orangeman, I'll give it to you. All you have to do is strike the first blow. [tr.] Significant numbers of people from Quebec had moved to Ontario. Although there were 200 000 Francophones in a population of 2.5 million, pressure was mounting to eliminate bilingual schools. The French Canadian cartoonist voices opposition to this idea.*

HEADED OUR WAY

THE COMET: I seem to be going in the right direction.

THE GREAT LAURIER–HAYS ELEPHANT ACT,
GOES HIGHER EACH YEAR.

Left. In Canada the 1900s were a time of unprecedented prosperity and record immigration. Halley's Comet, which appeared in 1910, observes the rush to western Canada. **Right.** *Costs escalated on the various railways which were under construction. Prime Minister Laurier is on the left and Charles Hayes, president of the Grand Trunk Pacific Railway, is riding on the elephant's trunk.*

PUTTING ON THE SCREWS
How the farmer benefits by a protective tariff.

CONTINENTAL UNION
Where the beaver would come in.

Left. As a result of the protective tariff against imported goods, Western Canadians paid higher prices for domestic manufactured goods from Eastern Canada. When Laurier visited the West in 1910 he was urged to reduce the protective tariff. *Right.* The cartoonist suggests that the elimination of the protective tariff would lead to Canada being swallowed by the United States.

THE FISCAL TUG-OF-WAR
Farmers' association vs. manufacturers' association.

Farmers favoured free trade, which resulted in lower prices for farm machinery and consumer goods; manufacturers favoured a protective tariff, which reduced competition and enabled them to charge more for their goods. This cartoon represents the forces at work in 1910. In actual practice, Sir John A. Macdonald's National Policy of 1878 had tipped the scales in favour of the manufacturers, and Laurier had done little to change the balance.

SIR WILFRID'S GREAT QUICK CHANGE ACT, OR ALL THINGS TO ALL MEN

Sir Wilfrid Laurier was the consummate politician.

A POLITICAL EPIDEMIC

William Taft was the president of the United States and Herbert Asquith was prime minister of Great Britain.

ON GUARD

Canadians were concerned about forest conservation.

EXTERMINATE IT!
The venomous snake in the grass

Large newspapers were often controlled by business interests who were strongly anti-union. This cartoon links organized crime to unions in order to discredit the labour movement.

NOXIOUS
Weed it out while young.

The Opium Act of 1908 had allowed the importing of opium for medical use only. The Opium and Drug Act of 1911 further restricted the possession of drugs such as opium and cocaine.

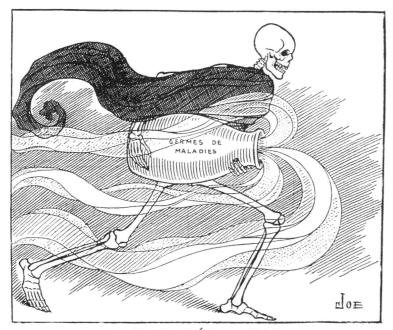

LA MORTALITÉ INFANTILLE
Quand va-t-on l'empêcher de venir répandre ses germes destructeurs sur nos pauvres petits?

TOO MANY TRICKS SPOIL THE JUGGLE.

Left. INFANT MORTALITY. *When will we stop it from spreading its destructive germs over our poor little ones? [tr.] A Quebec newspaper reported that one hundred and eighteen children under the age of five had died the previous week.* **Right.** *The juggler is Sir Wilfrid Laurier.*

CANADA'S HOUSE OF LORDS – THEIR VETO MUST GO

Political appointees to the Canadian Senate were often criticized for protecting the interests of monopolies and big business.

"LET THE FARMER HAVE HIS TURN."

AMERICAN FARMER: What's that I hear? 'Let the farmer have his turn!' Right you are. Just watch me when this door is opened!

American president Taft proposed a reciprocity treaty that would allow both Canadians and Americans to buy farm produce more cheaply. This Conservative cartoon warns that the Canadian market would be flooded with surplus American farm products.

This Liberal cartoon emphasizes the advantage President Taft's reciprocity treaty would give Canadian farmers, who would have access to a much larger market and receive higher prices for their goods.

"Some Day—PERHAPS," Says The Denver Times

ON COMMON GROUND

Left. In 1911 the speaker of the United States House of Representatives made a speech supporting free trade and predicting the annexation of Canada.
Right. Quebec nationalist Henri Bourassa feared that reciprocity would increase American influence in Canada. He also opposed Prime Minister Laurier's naval bill. He and federal Conservative leader Robert Borden formed an alliance in hope of defeating Laurier in the upcoming federal election.

AMBIDEXTERITY!
Mr. Borassa-Bourden, the headline artist of the Conservative vaudeville.

Opposition to Laurier's naval bill united the Conservative imperialists under Borden and the anti-imperialist nationalists under Bourassa. "Borassa-Bourden" is shown drawing caricatures of Sir Wilfrid Laurier, tailoring the criticism to suit the intended audience.

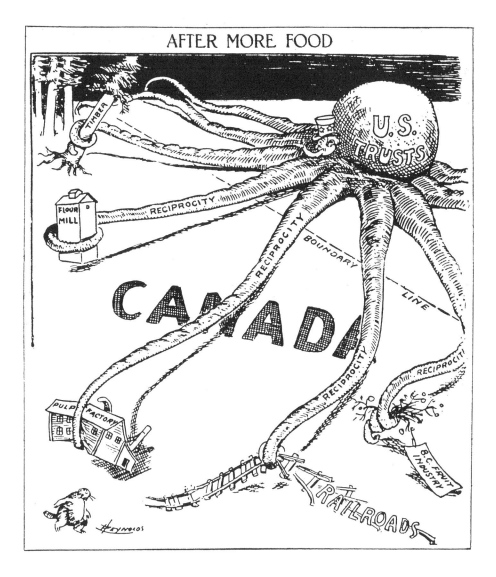

Left. Liberals criticized the Conservative tariff policy for favouring special interest groups. *Right*. Conservatives felt that removal of the tariff barrier would allow giant US businesses free access to Canadian resources, industries and transportation systems and result in economic takeover.

ALL THAT IS HOLDING HIM BACK

This Liberal cartoon suggests that the only thing preventing the government from adopting a free trade policy was the greed of wealthy businessmen.

THE TUG OF WAR

TARIFF WALL

THE GREAT RECIPROCITY GAME   HER MOVE

A DEATH-DEFYING LEAP

Upper left. *The cartoonist suggests that Laurier, pulling with Uncle Sam and US president Taft, is working against Canadian and British interests.* **Lower left.** *The Americans had basically opposed free trade since 1866. In the spring of 1911 they made Canadians an attractive offer. Tariffs were to be removed on some products and lowered but not eliminated on others.* **Right.** *This Conservative cartoon suggests that Canadians will replace dependence on Britain with dependence on the United States if they vote for reciprocity. The figures in the lower left corner are United States president William Taft and Sir Wilfrid Laurier.*

UNDER WHICH FLAG ?

Reciprocity was the major issue in the federal election of September 1911.

"COME ON SONNY, I'LL CATCH YOU"

LOOKING OUR WAY.

SIR WILFRID ARRIVES.

THE CUT DIRECT

ONE OF THE RESULTS OF THE RECIPROCITY VERDICT.

Facing page, left and upper right. The cartoonist suggests that reciprocity will lead to the annexation of Canada by the United States. *Facing page, lower right.* Sir Wilfrid Laurier visited Great Britain prior to the 1911 election. His reciprocity treaty was not well received. *This page.* In the election of September 1911, voters rejected Laurier's platform of reciprocity with the United States and elected Robert Borden.

ON THE ROCKS

COMING OVER LIKE SHEEP

Left. This cartoon predicts that Borden's alliance with Bourassa will make it difficult for him to deal with the Canadian naval question. As Bourassa's group did not hold the balance of power in the House of Commons, Borden was in fact able to proceed with his own naval bill. *Right.* Canada's wheat production skyrocketed from 8 million bushels in 1896 to 231 million bushels in 1911. In 1911 more than 330 000 people arrived in Canada, with 30 per cent coming from the United States.

DECORATIONS AND LOUD CHEERS FROM SUFFRAGETTES
"An Ottawa magistrate has ruled that a wife may use an axe on her husband in extreme cases."

The cartoonist has used a judicial decision to make fun of the women's movement.

WIFEY IS IN JAIL

Suffragists believed in extending the vote to women. Some female members of the suffrage movement were militant in the methods they used to further their cause, and a few were imprisoned.

THE BIG NOISE

Henri Bourassa resigned from the House of Commons in 1907 to serve in the Quebec Legislative Assembly. In 1912 he left politics to devote full time to his daily newspaper Le Devoir. *He used the paper to promote Canadian autonomy, minority rights, provincial rights and loyalty to British ideals.*

THE BONE OF CONTENTION

OLD MAN ONTARIO: Well, if you're aimin' to please me, Mr. Whitney,
you'll cut the bone out altogether.

UNDER ONE FLAG

"You take away our country, teach our men to fight for you, and preach to
us of liberty, yet we may not live even in the outskirts of your Empire."

Left. In 1912 Ontario ended its bilingual school system in an attempt to assimilate its French-speaking citizens. The use of English became compulsory
for all children after the first year of schooling. James Whitney was premier of Ontario at the time. *Right.* The continuous passage law of 1908 stopped
women from India from joining their husbands in Canada. Some women who returned to Canada with their husbands were given orders of expulsion.

THE DANCE OF OPPORTUNITY

LOOKS PROSPEROUS FOR WESTERN CANADA!

*Left. Canada was slow to respond to trading opportunities in South America. **Right.** The settlement of western Canada fueled railway expansion which helped stimulate the nation's economy.*

IF All Europe Becomes Involved In General War Over the Spoils of the Conflict In the Balkans

Canadians were well aware of the growing tensions in Europe evidenced by the 1912–13 conflict in the Balkan peninsula, between the Adriatic and Black Seas. Britain still controlled Canada's foreign policy, and if Britain went to war Canada would automatically be at war as well.

**A PROMINENT MEMBER OF THE CANADIAN
HOME MARKET ASSOCIATION IN ACTION**

Right. The British passenger ship Titanic *struck an iceberg and sank off the coast of Newfoundland on April 15, 1912, with the loss of more than 1600 lives. Many women and children survived, thanks to the heroism of the men who chose to go down with the ship rather than to take places in the inadequate number of lifeboats. The cartoonist expresses admiration for the British race.*

TO THE RESCUE – GUESS WHO'S GOING TO BE RESCUED!

Richard McBride was premier and William Bowser attorney general of British Columbia during the coal miners' strike of 1912–14. The government actively supported the mining interests.

HAS IT EVER HAPPENED TO YOU??

COLLECTING THE THANKSGIVING DINNER

These cartoons illustrate some of the problems encountered by working people.

OUT OF YOUR PLENTY REMEMBER THE POOR
CHILDREN: "What do we get for Christmas, mamma?"

News item – An anxious mother seeks information of her daughter, who has been missing several days.

"Oh, God, that bread should be so dear, and flesh and blood so cheap."
Thomas Hood

Left. Not everyone benefited from the boom years of the early 1900s. The steady influx of immigrants kept wages low and poverty was a problem for many. **Right.** Poverty was one problem contributing to "white slavery" or prostitution.

Subsidized railways, tariff-protected manufacturers and bankers were often the target of the Grain Grower's Guide, *a prairie newspaper. Having enjoyed a fine dinner, the railway magnate, the manufacturer and the banker generously decide to pass the skeleton over to the farmer who raised the turkey.*

An Uneasy Seat

A western Canadian cartoon expressing strong opposition to Borden's decision to continue with a protective tariff.

OF COURSE IT HURTS!

Discriminatory railway freight rates were a major western Canadian grievance. It cost more to send manufactured goods from west to east than vice-versa, making it difficult for western Canadian industries to compete with those in the east.

The Big Interests Octopus of the East is Reaching Out For Saskatchewan

With the advent of Premier Borden to power last September, the Big Interests Octopus from its lair in Toronto commenced to reach out boldly to fasten its blood-sucking tentacles upon the people of Canada. Now the Beast is hovering over Saskatchewan prepared to encircle this province. Should Saskatchewan by any chance succumb to it and a Borden-Haultain Government be placed in power, then nothing could prevent the Octopus from working its will upon the common people of Canada. The fight today is a fight between the Common People and the Big Interests Octopus, and for the Common People it is a fight for very life.

The cartoonist voices western Canadian fears of Prime Minister Borden's protective tariff, which enriched eastern Canadian industries at the expense of the rest of the country. Frederick Haultain was the leader of the Provincial Rights party in Saskatchewan.

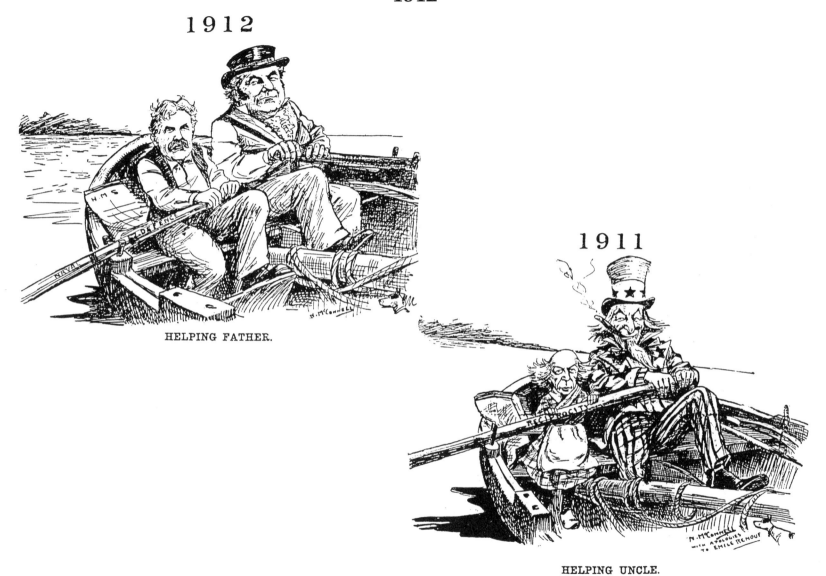

HELPING FATHER.

HELPING UNCLE.

In December 1912 Borden proposed a bill to give Britain thirty-five million dollars to build three dreadnoughts (battleships). Borden's pro-British naval bill (left) is contrasted to Laurier's earlier "pro-American" reciprocity policy (right).

THE GIFT OF THE SEA-KING'S DAUGHTER.

RÉSULTAT DE L'ALLIANCE TORY-NATIONALISTE
BORDEN: Veuillez accepter, John Bull, $35 000 000 pour votre marine de la part des Canayens. Voilà le résultat de l'Alliance Tory-Nationaliste. Qu'en pense le "Maître" maintenant.

Left. Prime Minister Borden's bill to support Britain's naval expansion gained the approval of the British press (this cartoon was published in Punch). *Right.* **RESULT OF THE TORY-NATIONALIST ALLIANCE.** *BORDEN: John Bull, be so good as to accept $35 000 000 from Canadians for your navy. What do you think of the Tory-Nationalist Alliance now? [tr.] Quebec nationalists disliked Borden's naval policy just as much as they disliked Laurier's, feeling that both threatened Canadian autonomy.*

THE PUPPET

Borden told the people of Quebec that his proposal to support the British navy would lessen the chance of Canadian sailors losing their lives. In this cartoon Borden, holding the three proposed dreadnoughts, is portrayed as a puppet controlled by Quebec.

TWO SIDES TO EVERY QUESTION

The naval question was a turning point in the development of Canadian independence. The Liberal proposal favoured a Canadian-controlled defence system and a greater say in foreign policy. The Conservative proposal favoured the status quo – a British-controlled defence and foreign policy.

THE REAL EMERGENCY

Prime Minister Borden was caught between two opposing factions, the "jingo-imperialists" of Ontario (who favoured supporting the British navy) and the nationalists of Quebec (who feared that support for Britain might lead to Canadian involvement in British conflicts). A commentary which accompanied the cartoon stated that the "real" emergency was not Britain's need for aid but Borden's need to satisfy both groups.

A CHOICE

"The Ottawa folks 's sot on me havin' th' Johnny Bull shape."

The Conservative bill to support an imperial navy would be passed by the House of Commons but defeated in the Liberal-controlled Senate, which supported a Canadian navy. Reliance on the United States for protection (the Monroe Doctrine) was not a serious option.

A REAL "EMERGENCY"

Cannot the speller be induced to leave the political sideshow and devote himself to the solving of the really vital issue?

MAY THE ECLIPSE BECOME TEE-TOTAL.

Left. The man on the soap box (the sideshow "speller") is Prime Minister Robert Borden. Most people were far more interested in the cost of living than they were in his proposal to buy three ships for the British navy. **Upper right.** The Women's Christian Temperance Union continued to press for prohibition. **Lower right.** The eight-hour day was one objective of workers at this time.

THE MOVING PICTURES AND OUR CANADIAN CHILDREN
They are regaled with pictures of US naval manoeuvres labelled *Our Navy*.

Canadians were concerned about their national identity and worried about American cultural influences.

THE REAL SANTA CLAUS

A REMINDER
MRS. VANCOUVER: Remember, you men are hired to *clean* this city, not merely to move its filth from one spot to another.

Upper left. Women who worked in factories or who did piece work at home were often paid very low wages for long hours of work. *Lower left.* This cartoon, published in a socialist newspaper, suggests that low wages forced women into prostitution. **Right.** British Columbia attorney general William Bowser and Vancouver mayor T.S. Baxter deal with the "social evil" of prostitution by moving it from one district to another. Mrs. Vancouver demands that they eliminate the problem.

"I VIEW WITH INDULGENT CALM..."

Left. Richard McBride (in the background) was premier of British Columbia from 1903 until 1915. The cartoon criticizes him for not protecting the province from land speculators and exploiters of her natural resources. *Right.* A stereotypical Montrealer expresses concern over water pollution.

When a Feller Needs a Friend :: *By Briggs*

" A VOTE FOR MOTHER IS A VOTE FOR A BETTER WORLD FOR ME DAD "

Left. *The campaign for female suffrage continued.* **Right.** *Justice seemed blind to the plight of women and other disadvantaged groups who sought the right to vote.*

PEACE HATH HER HEROES

TO THE MEMORY OF 1220 WORKERS WHO MET DEATH IN CANADIAN INDUSTRIAL PLANTS DURING 1912

Working conditions in factories and mines and on the railroads were particularly dangerous. In 1912 industrial accidents caused the death of more than 1200 workers and injured many more.

THE PRIVILEGED MINER

DEATH (to Colliery Proprietor): So long as you allow me the run of your pits, so long as you drop in for these extras, d'you see? You turn your back on me and listen to those fellows behind, and your extras stop. It is for you to choose. (Vancouver Island is a voice only too painfully clear telling us what the Capitalist's choice is.)

In 1910 thirty-two miners were killed in a Vancouver Island coal mine. A committee of workers who launched a complaint about safety conditions were fired, touching off the coal miners' strike of 1912–14. This cartoon from a labour newspaper charges that mine operators were willing to risk workers' lives for the sake of profits.

A DEODORIZER NEEDED

MR. BORDEN: The whitewash hides most of the dirt beneath, but the smell seems as bad as ever.

THE TALE OF THE UNEMPLOYED

CAPITALIST (indignantly): What does this mean? LABORER: We want work. CAPITALIST: I have none to offer you. Go and see the Mayor at the City Hall. When everything is booming again I can use all of you and more, too. But not now. Drive on, James.

Left. The BC coal miners' strike ended in defeat for the workers in 1914. *Right.* Poor working conditions, long hours of work, low wages, the high cost of living and lack of relief for the unemployed made the trade union movement attractive to workers.

Left. *Job opportunities for women expanded and the number of women in the paid workforce increased. Even though their wages were generally very low, women now had an alternative to marriage.* **Right.** *Governments at this time were investing heavily in publicly-owned hydroelectric, telephone and transportation systems. Government ownership was seen as threatening by many businessmen.*

NOT A FREE AGENT

PREMIER BORDEN: My dear fellow, I would like to come to your relief! Really, I would, but – you see how it is.

High food costs were a continuing problem for consumers.

PLAYING THE FAVORITE

Western farmers were unsuccessful in getting the prime minister to eliminate or lower the protective tariff.

CLEANING UP THE FRONT YARD

Left. Prime Minister Robert Borden supported racist policies designed to limit Asian immigration to Canada. **Right and opposite.** On May 23, 1914, 376 immigrants from India arrived in Vancouver aboard the Komagata Maru. Few were allowed to land, and after a minor skirmish in Burrard Inlet the ship left for India on July 23.

ONE DARK CLOUD REMOVED

VANCOUVER

AS IT MIGHT HAVE BEEN
What if a lump of coal had hit our navy!

Left. The Canadian navy consisted of two aged destroyers. The Rainbow, *stationed on the west coast, forced the* Komagata Maru *to return to India. The eastern Canadian cartoonist reveals both a stereotypical view of the potential immigrants and a Conservative bias in his put-down of the Canadian navy.*
Right. An astonishing 400 870 immigrants had entered Canada in 1913, when Canada's population was around eight million. Although only a small percentage came from Asia, they were singled out by Canadians who worried about absorbing so many immigrants.

WE DON'T LIKE THE SMELL OF IT EITHER ANDREW.

Ontario member of parliament Andrew Broder introduced a bill to prohibit the manufacture, sale or use of cigarettes in Canada.

LA DERNIÈRE DE BORDEN

Grace au parti Libéral, Borden n'a pas donné à l'Angleterre nos millions. Le voilà maintenant qu'il veut jeter les canayens dans la gueule du lion Britannique. Décidément il est temps qu'on fasse des élections.

Left. BORDEN'S LATEST. *The Liberal Party stopped Borden from giving England our millions, but now he wants to throw Canadians into the jaws of the British lion. It is definitely time for an election. [tr.] The Liberal-controlled Senate had prevented Borden from giving Britain thirty-five million dollars for her navy. The cartoon predicts Borden will send troops to Europe if a war erupts.* **Upper right.** *This cartoon was published the day Great Britain declared war on Germany.* **Lower right.** *Many French Canadians wondered why they should fight in Europe when their rights were being denied in Canada.*

FLOCKING TO EUROPE.

EUROPE

ONTARIO VS QUEBEC

ANSWERING THE CALL
" The whelps of the lion are joining their sire."

This chauvinistic drawing captured the mood of many Canadians. It was reproduced in newspapers throughout the British Empire.

THE ANGEL OF DEATH IS ABROAD IN EUROPE

OLD FRIENDS MEET

These anti-war cartoons were printed in the Grain Grower's Guide *soon after the outbreak of war. The tremendous support for the war on the prairies later forced the cartoonist to change his bias.*

OPPRESSION OR FREEDOM

TWO OF A KIND

Left. This cartoon was published in a Liberal newspaper. **Right.** The cartoonist reveals a strong bias against both the German Kaiser and native people, comparing the cruelty of the Kaiser to that of the stereotypical Iroquois warrior.

"THE MAD DOG OF EUROPE"

BOURASSA'S ONE-MAN BAND

THE RECRUITING SERGEANT: If you want that flute to be heard, Henri, why don't you stop banging the drum?

*Left. John Bull (Britain) is portrayed in a heroic role, defending the small nation of Belgium against German aggression. **Right.** Quebec nationalist Henri Bourassa was not opposed to Canada's participation in the war; he even encouraged the recruitment of a French Canadian regiment, The Royal 22nd (the "Van Doos"). However, his support was cautious and French Canadian enthusiasm for the war quickly cooled off.*

NOT COMMANDEERED, BUT VOLUNTEERED

JOHN BULL: Well, the young 'uns won't see me run short of provisions anyway!

Most Canadians enthusiastically supported the war effort.

SHOULDER TO SHOULDER

With flags waving, thirty thousand Canadian troops sailed for England at the beginning of October 1914 to join Britain and the other colonies in their common cause.

Appendix

Canadian Prime Ministers 1867–1914

Rt. Hon. Sir John A. Macdonald	Liberal Conservative	1867 – 1873
Hon. Alexander Mackenzie	Liberal	1873 – 1878
Rt. Hon. Sir John A. Macdonald	Liberal Conservative	1878 – 1891
Hon. Sir John Abbott	Liberal Conservative	1891 – 1892
Rt. Hon. Sir John Thompson	Liberal Conservative	1892 – 1894
Hon. Sir Mackenzie Bowell	Conservative	1894 – 1896
Rt. Hon. Sir Charles Tupper	Conservative	1896
Rt. Hon. Sir Wilfrid Laurier	Liberal	1896 – 1911
Rt. Hon. Sir Robert Borden	Conservative	1911 – 1920

Leaders of the Official Opposition 1869–1914

The Hon. Edward Blake	Liberal	1869 – 1871
The Hon. Alexander Mackenzie	Liberal	1872 – 1873
The Rt. Hon. Sir John A. Macdonald	Conservative	1873 – 1878
The Hon. Alexander Mackenzie	Liberal	1878 – 1880
The Hon. Edward Blake	Liberal	1880 – 1887
The Rt. Sir. Wilfrid Laurier	Liberal	1887 – 1896
The Rt. Hon. Sir Charles Tupper	Conservative	1896 – 1900
The Rt. Hon. Sir Robert Borden	Conservative	1901 – 1911
The Rt. Hon. Sir Wilfrid Laurier	Liberal	1911 – 1919

Bibliography

Books

Barbeau, Marius. *Côté The Wood Carver*. Toronto, The Ryerson Press, 1943.

Barbeau, Marius. *Henri Julien*. Toronto, The Ryerson Press, 1941.

Bengough, J.W. *A Caricature History of Canadian Politics*. Toronto, Grip, 1886.

Bengough, J.W. *Cartoons of the Campaign Dominion of Canada General Election 1900*. Toronto, Poole, 1900.

Bengough, J.W. *Chalk Talks*. Toronto, Musson, 1922.

Canadian Cartoon and Caricature. Toronto, Art Gallery of Toronto, 1969.

Canadian Illustrated News 1869–1883: Canada's first national magazine. Toronto, McClelland and Stewart, n.d.

Cook, Ramsay, "'The Ragged Reformer' – J. W. Bengough: The Caricaturist as Social Critic," in W. H. New, *A Political Art:*

Essays and Images in Honour of George Woodcock. Vancouver, UBC Press, 1978.

Dempsey, Hugh. *Western Alienation in Perspective*. Calgary, Glenbow Museum, 1981.

Desbarats, Peter and Terry Mosher. *The Hecklers*. Toronto, McClelland and Stewart, 1979.

Laurier Does Things. 1900.

Racey, A.C. *The Englishman in Canada*. 1880.

Ryan, Alonzo. *Caricature Politique au Canada*. Montreal, Dominion, 1904.

Seguin, R.L. *L'Esprit revolutionaire dans l'art quebecois*. Montreal, Parit Pris, 1972.

To Canada. Ottawa, Minister of the Interior, Hon. Clifford Sifton, 1903.

Werthman, William C. *Canada in Cartoon*. Fredericton, Brunswick Press, 1967.

Periodicals

American Monthly Review of Reviews (New York), L'Avenir (Montreal), *The British Columbia Federationist* (Vancouver), *British Columbia Saturday Night* (Vancouver), *The British Columbian* (New Westminster), *Le Canada* (Montreal), *The Canadian Illustrated News* (Montreal), *The Canadian Liberal Monthly* (Ottawa), *The Canadian Magazine* (Toronto), *Le Canard* (Montreal), *Caricature Politique au Canada* (Montreal), *Citizen and Country* (Toronto), *Le Combat* (Montreal), *Le Cultivateur* (Montreal), *The Daily Herald* (Calgary), *Daily Klondike Nugget* (Dawson City), *The Daily Mail and Empire* (Toronto), *Les Débats* (Montreal), *Diogenes* (Toronto), *The Dominion Illustrated* (Toronto), *The Edmonton Journal, The Evening Telegram* (Toronto), *The Eye Opener* (Calgary), *Le Farceur* (Montreal), *The Globe* (Toronto), *The Grain Growers' Guide* (Winnipeg), *Grinchuckle* (Toronto), *Grip* (Toronto), *Le Grognard* (Montreal), *The Halifax Herald, The Hearthstone* (Montreal), *Le Journal* (Montreal), *Manitoba Morning Free Press* (Winnipeg), *The Montreal Daily Herald, The Montreal Daily Star, The Moon* (Toronto), *The Morning Leader* (Regina), *The News* (Toronto), *L'Opinion Publique* (Montreal), *Le Perroquet* (Montreal), *Punch* (London), *Punch in Canada* (Toronto), *La Scie – The Saw* (Quebec), *The Standard* (Montreal), *The Sun* (Vancouver), *The Templar Quarterly* (Toronto), *The Toronto Daily Star, The Toronto Evening News, The Toronto News, Toronto Saturday Night, The Toronto World, The Vancouver Daily Province, The Vancouver Daily World, The Vancouver World, Le Vrai Canard* (Montreal), *The Witness* (Montreal), *The Week* (Victoria), *Western Clarion* (Vancouver), *Winnipeg Free Press, Winnipeg Tribune*.

Film

The Hecklers: Two Centuries of Canadian history, from a political cartoonist's point of view. Montreal, National Film Board of Canada, 1981.

Credits and Acknowledgements

Cover: The front cover is based on a cartoon by Alonzo Ryan which appears on page 143; the figures on the back cover are from cartoons by Owen Staples (*TET*, 1903) and J. W. Bengough (*Grip*, Jan 1894).

Cartoons on composite pages are listed in the following order: upper left, lower left, upper right, lower right. Abbreviations follow credits.

vii *Grip*, May 1882; **1** PAC C41067; **2** *Punch*, 1846; **3** *Punch*, Jan 1846; *Punch*, Mar 1846; **4** *PIC*, May 1849; *PIC*, Sep 1849; **5** *PIC*, Oct 1849; *PIC*, 1849; **6** *LS*, Dec 1864; **7** *LS*, Dec 1864; **8** *LP*, Jan 1865; **9** *LS*, Feb 1865; *LS*, Jan 1866; *LS*, Oct 1865; **10** *LP*, Feb 1865; **11** *LS*, Nov 1865; **12** *LS*, Apr 1866; *LS*, Mar 1866; **13** *LS*, Apr 1866; **14** 1867[?]; **15** *Dio*, Nov 1868; **16** *Dio*, Dec 1868; **17** *Grin*, Sep 1869; *Dio*, Jun 1869; **18** *Dio*, Nov 1869; **19** *CIN*, Jan 1870; *CIN*, Jun 1870; **20** *CIN*, Jul 1870; **21** *CIN*, Jun 1870; **22** *CIN*, Sep 1870; **23** *CIN*, Sep 1871; **24** *Punch*, Nov 1872; **25** *CIN*, Aug 1873; **26** *Grip*, Aug 1873; *Grip*, Sep 1873; **27** *Grip*, Apr 1874; *CIN*, Oct 1874; **28** *LOP*, Aug 1875; *CIN*, Apr 1875; **29** *CIN*, Aug 1875; **30** *CIN*, Sept 1876; **31** *CIN*, Apr 1876; **32** *LCa*, Nov 1878; *CIN*, Sep 1878; **33** *LCa*, Feb 1879; detail from *Grip*, Jan 1879; **34** *LCa*, Dec 1879; **35** *CIN*, Apr 1879; **36** *LCa*, Apr 1880; **37** *LCa*, Feb 1880; *The Englishman in Canada*, 1880; **38** *CIN*, Oct 1880; **39** *LVC*, Apr 1880; **40** *Grip*, Dec 1880; *LOP*, Dec 1880; **41** *LCa*, Dec 1881; **42** *LCa*, Aug 1881; *LVC*, Jan 1881; *LCa*, Apr 1881; **43** *LCa*, Aug 1881; **44** *CIN*, Dec 1881; **45** *Grip*, Feb 1882; **46** *LCa*, May 1882; **47** *LCa*, Aug 1882; **48** *Grip*, Mar 1882; **49** *Grip*, Mar 1882; **50** *Grip*, Aug 1883; **51** *Grip*, Feb 1883; **52** *Grip*, Nov 1883; **53** *Grip*, Nov 1883; **54** *Grip*, Oct 1884; **55** *Grip*, Jun 1884; **56** *Grip*, Jan 1885; **57** *Grip*, Mar 1885; **58** *TTEN*, Jun 1885; **59** *LCa*, Jul 1885; **60** *Grip*, Apr 1885; *LCa*, May 1885; **61** *Grip*, May 1885; **62** *Grip*, Aug 1885; *Grip*, Sep 1885; *LCa*, Dec 1885; **63** *LCa*, Nov 1885; *Grip*, Nov 1885; **64** *Grip*, Sep 1885; **65** *Grip*, Jul 1885; *Grip*, Sep 1885; **66** *TTEN*, May 1885; **67** *Grip*, Dec 1886; **68** *Grip*, Nov 1887; **69** *Grip*, Jul 1887; *Grip*, Jan 1887; **70** *Grip*, Mar 1887; *Grip*, Feb 1887; **71** *Grip*, Feb 1888; *Grip*, Jan 1888; **72** *TNYW*, reprinted in *TMDS*, Dec 1888; *Grip*, Apr 1888; **73** *Grip*, Feb 1890; *Grip*, Sep 1890; **74** *Grip*, Dec 1890; *Grip*, Feb 1890; **75** *Grip*, Feb 1890; **76** *TDI*, Jan 1891; **77** PAC, 1891; *Grip*, Nov 1891; **78** *TG*, Feb 1892; *Grip*, Mar 1892; **79** *TMDS*, Dec 1893; **80** *TTW*, Jan 1893; **81** *LCa*, Jul 1894; **82** *TTW*, Sep 1894; *Grip*, 1894; **83** *Grip*, 1894; **84** *LCa*, Aug 1895; *TTQ*, Nov 1895; **85** *LCa*, May 1895; **86** *LCa*, Mar 1895; *TET*, Jan 1895; **87** *LCa*, Feb 1896; *LCa*,

May 1896; **88** *TDME*, Jun 1896; *TET*, Oct 1896; **89** *TG*, Jul 1896; **90** *TET*, Aug 1897; *TTW*, Jan 1897; **91** *TET*, Jul 1897; *TG*, Sep 1897; **92** *TG*, Jan 1898; **93** *TTW*, Dec 1898; *TTW*, Apr 1898; **94** *TG*, May 1898; **95** *TG*, Jan 1899; **96** *TET*, Jun 1899; *TDME*, Jul 1899; **97** *Jou*, reprinted in *TCM*, Oct 1899; *LCa*, Sep 1899; **98** MTPL 899 02; *TMDS*, Oct 1899; **99** *TMDS*, Oct 1899; **100** *LCa*, Jun 1900; **101** *MT*, reprinted in *AMRR*, Apr 1900; *TMDS*, Jan 1900; **102** *LD*, Jan 1900; *LCa*, Jan 1900; **103** *LCa*, Sep 1900; **104** *TET*, Aug 1900; *TMDS*, Mar 1900; **105** *TMDS*, Mar 1900; *TET*, Aug 1900; **106** *Cartoons of the Campaign*, 1900; **107** *TTW*, Aug 1900; **108** *LCa*, Aug 1900; **109** *LCa*, Jun 1901; **110** *LCa*, Aug 1901; **111** *LD*, Oct 1901; **112** *TMDS*, Sep 1901; *LCa*, July 1901; **113** *LCa*, Nov 1901; **114** *LJ*, Mar 1902; *TSN*, Nov 1902; **115** *TM*, Jul 1902; *TMDS*, May 1902; **116** *LJ*, Mar 1902; *TMDS*, Nov 1902; **117** *TM*, 1902; **118** *CC*, May 1902; *TTW*, Sep 1902; **119** *TM*, Aug 1902; **120** *TM*, Nov 1902; **121** *To Canada*, 1903; **122** *LCa*, May 1903; *LCa*, Feb 1903; **123** *To Canada*, 1903; **124** *TM*, Apr 1903; **125** *TMDS*, Sep 1903; *LCa*, Sep 1903; **126** *TTW*, Oct 1903; **127** *TSN*, Oct 1903; *LCo*, Nov 1903; **128** *TMDS*, Nov 1903; **129** *NA*, reprinted in *AMRR*, Dec 1903; **130** *LCa*, Sep 1903; *LCo*, Nov 1903; **131** *LCa*, Dec 1903; *LD*, Apr 1903; **132** *LCan*, May 1903; *LCa*, May 1903; **133** *TSN*, May 1903; *TMDS*, Jun 1903; **134** *TTW*, Sep 1903; *TMDS*, Jan 1903; **135** *LCu*, May, 1903; *TTW*, Dec 1903; **136** *TM*, Jun 1903; **137** *LCa*, May 1903; *LCa*, Sep 1903; **138** *LCa*, Jun 1904; *LCa*, Aug 1904; **139** *LCa*, Dec 1903; *LCa*, Jan 1904; **140** *LCa*, Feb 1904; *TSN*, Mar 1904; **141** *CPC*, 1904; *TSN*, Dec 1904; **142** *Laurier Does Things*, 1904; PAC C17193; **143** *LCa*, Jul 1904; *LCa*, Mar 1904; **144** *TN*, Mar 1905; **145** *TSN*, Mar 1905; *LCa*, May 1905; **146** *TEO*, Sep 1905; **147** *TSN*, Feb 1905; *LCa*, Apr 1905; **148** *TW*, Apr 1905; **149** *LCa*, Sep 1906; *LCa*, Oct 1906; **150** *LCa*, Nov 1906; **151** *LCa*, Apr 1907; **152** *TMDS*, Feb 1907; **153** *LCa*, Sep 1907; *Jou*, reprinted in *AMRR*, Oct 1907; **154** *TDH*, Jan 1907; *BCSS*, Aug 1907 (VPL 39046); **155** *TG*, Oct 1907; **156** *TMDS*, Mar 1908; *TVDP*, Mar 1908; **157** *TTW*, Mar 1908; *LCa*, Mar 1908; **158** *TET*, Jul 1909; *TTW*, Mar 1909; **159** *TTDS*, Feb 1909; **160** *Sun*, reprinted in *AMRR*, Jan 1909; **161** *TGGG*, Sep 1910 (GA); **162** *TEO*, Jan 1910 (GA); *TVDP*, Jan 1910; **163** *TTW*, Sep 1910; *LCa*, Oct 1910; **164** *TVDP*, Apr 1910; *TN*, Aug 1910; **165** *TGGG*, Apr 1910; *TET*, Aug 1910; **166** *TG*, Dec 1910; **167** *TN*, Sep 1910; **168** *TN*, Nov 1910; **169** *TMH*, Jan 1911; **170** *TMDS*, Dec 1911; **171** *TMDS*, Jan 1911; **172** *LCa*, Jul 1911; *TN*, Jun 1911; **173** *TGGG*, Aug 1911 (GA); **174** *TMDS*, Aug 1911; **175** *TVW*, Jul 1911; **176** *EJ*, Jun

1911; *TMH*, Sep 1911; **177** *TG*, Aug 1911; **178** *TVW*, Aug 1911; *TVDP*, Apr 1911; **179** *TVW*, Jul 1911; **180** *TN*, Sep 1911; *TSN*, Sep 1911; *TVDP*, Aug 1911; **181** *TTDS*, Sep 1911; **182** *TVDP*, Sep 1911; *TN*, Aug 1911; *TN*, May 1911; **183** *TMH*, Sep 1911; *TMH*, Oct 1911; **184** *TVW*, Nov 1911; *TVDP*, Aug 1911; **185** *TMDS*, Jul 1911; **186** *TVDP*, Mar 1912; **187** *TTW*, Apr 1912; **188** *TTW*, Apr 1912; *TMH*, May 1912; **189** *TVDP*, Apr 1912; *TVW*, Jan 1912; **190** *THH*, Nov 1912; **191** *TGGG*, Jun 1912; *TW*, May 1912; **192** *TBCF*, Nov 1912; **193** *TVDW*, Oct 1912; **194** *TVW*, Dec 1912; *TVDW*, Oct 1912; **195** *TGGG*, Dec 1912; **196** *TGGG*, Sep 1912; **197** *TML*, Jul 1912; **198** *TML*, Jun 1912; **199** *TN*, Jul 1912; **200** *Punch*, Dec 1912; *LCa*, Dec 1912; **201** *TML*, Dec 1912; **202** *TTW*, Jan 1913; **203** *TCLM*, Sep 1913; **204** *TTW*, Apr 1913; **205** *TSu*, Dec 1913; *TML*, Oct 1913; *TBCF*, Oct 1913; **206** *THH*, May 1913; **207** *THH*, Dec 1913; *WC*, Aug 1913; *TSu*, Dec 1913; **208** *TSu*, Aug 1913; *TML*, Dec 1913; **209** *TMDH*, Nov 1913; **210** *TML*, Dec 1913; **211** *TBCF*, Nov 1913; **212** *TSu*, Mar 1914; *TBC*, Jan 1914; **213** *TTW*, Feb 1914; *THH*, May 1914; **214** *TML*, Jan 1914; **215** *TEO*, Apr 1914 (GA); **216** *TTW*, Apr 1914; *TML*, May 1914; **217** *TMDS*, Jul 1914; *TTW*, Jun 1914; **218** *THH*, Feb 1914; **219** *LCa*, Jun 1914; *THH*, Aug 1914; *LCa*, Jul 1914; **220** *TVDP*, Aug 1914; **221** *TGGG*, Aug 1914; **222** *TCLM*, Aug 1914; *TSt*, Sep 1914; **223** *TSt*, Aug 1914; *TET*, Oct 1914; **224** *TCLM*, Oct 1914; **225** *TGGG*, Nov 1914; **226** PIO.

Abbreviations

AMRR *American Monthly Review of Reviews* (New York); *BCSS* *B.C. Saturday Sunset* (Vancouver); *CIN* *Canadian Illustrated News* (Montreal); *CC* *Citizen and Country* (Toronto); *CPC* *Caricature Politique au Canada* (Montreal); *Dio* *Diogenes* (Toronto); *EJ* *Edmonton Journal;* **GA** Glenbow Archives (Calgary); *Grin* *Grinchuckle* (Toronto); *Grip* (Toronto); *Jou* *Journal* (Detroit); *LCan* *Le Canada* (Montreal); *LCa* *Le Canard* (Montreal); *LCo* *Le Combat* (Montreal); *LCu* *Le Cultivateur* (Montreal); *LD* *Les Debats* (Montreal); *LJ* *Le Journal* (Montreal); *LOP* *L'Opinion Publique* (Montreal); *LP* *Le Perroquet* (Montreal); *LS* *La Scie* (Quebec); *LVC* *Le Vrai Canard* (Montreal); *MT* *Minneapolis Tribune;* **MTPL** Metropolitan Toronto Public Library; *NA* *North American* (Philadelphia); **PAC** Public Archives of Canada; **PIO** Public Information Office (Ottawa); *Punch* (London); *PIC* *Punch in Canada* (Toronto); *Sun* (Baltimore); *TBCF*

The British Columbia Federationist (Vancouver); *TBC* *The British Columbian* (New Westminster); *TCLM* *The Canadian Liberal Monthly* (Ottawa); *TCM* *The Canadian Magazine* (Toronto); *TDI* *The Dominion Illustrated* (Toronto); *TDH* *The Daily Herald* (Calgary); *TDME* *The Daily Mail and Empire* (Toronto); *TEO* *The Eye Opener* (Calgary); *TET* *The Evening Telegram* (Toronto); *TG* *The Globe* (Toronto); *TGGG* *The Grain Growers' Guide* (Winnipeg); *THH* *The Halifax Herald*; *TM* *The Moon* (Toronto); *TMDH* *The Montreal Daily Herald*; *TMDS* *The Montreal Daily Star*; *TMH* *The Montreal Herald*; *TML* *The Morning Leader* (Regina); *TN* *The News* (Toronto); *TSN* *Toronto Saturday Night*; *TNYW* *The New York World*; *TSt* *The Standard* (Montreal); *TSu* *The Sun* (Vancouver); *TTDS* *The Toronto Daily Star*; *TTEN* *The Toronto Evening News*; *TTN* *The Toronto News*; *TTQ* *The Templar Quarterly* (Toronto); *TTW* *The Toronto World*; *TVDP* *The Vancouver Daily Province*; *TVDW* *The Vancouver Daily World*; *TVW* *The Vancouver World*; *TW* *The Week* (Victoria); **VPL** Vancouver Public Library; *WC* *Western Clarion* (Vancouver).

Acknowledgements

Assistance with research was provided by the following institutions: Glenbow Archives, Calgary; Metropolitan Toronto Public Library; Provincial Archives of British Columbia, Victoria; Public Archives of Canada, Ottawa (with special thanks to Susan North and Jennifer Devine); University of British Columbia Library, Vancouver; Vancouver Public Library.

Every attempt has been made to trace copyright ownership and credit sources correctly. The authors would be pleased to hear of any errors or omissions. Cartoons by C. W. Jefferys on pages 119 and 136 are reproduced with the permission of the C. W. Jefferys Estate Archive, Toronto. Cartoons by Owen Staples ("Rostap") on pages 86, 88, 90, 91, 96, 104, 105, 158, 165, and 223 are reprinted with the kind permission of Mr. Rod Staples.

Helpful suggestions regarding the manuscript were provided by Steve Bailey, John Collins, Cynthia Grenier, Jocelyn Per and Gordon Smith. The authors would particularly like to acknowledge the invaluable criticism and encouragement given by John Collins and Gordon Smith.

Index

public ownership 213

Quebec 6, 8, 34, 46, 62, 66, 73, 90, 110

racism 35, 108–09, 112, 149, 153–55, 216–17, 222 (see also continuous passage, head tax)
railways 18, 117, 137–38, 164, 189, 195, 197 (see also Canadian Pacific Railway)
Rebellion Losses Bill 4
Rebellion of 1837 4, 31, 62, 102, 111
Red River colony 19
remittance men 37
Riel, Louis 22, 27, 60–63, 66
Riel Rebellion of 1885 60–63
Roosevelt, Theodore 135, 160
Royal 22nd regiment (Van Doos) 223
Russia 95, 120

St. Pierre 116, 139
San Juan dispute 24
Saskatchewan 52, 144–46, 198
Scott, Thomas 22
Senate 67, 96, 158–59, 173
separate schools
  Alberta 144-46
  Manitoba 74, 75, 81, 82, 86, 87, 187
  Ontario 163, 187–88
  Saskatchewan 144–45
settlement of the west 43, 48, 58, 59, 142–43, 164
Seward, William 14
Sifton, Clifford 94, 108, 120, 121, 144
Smith, Donald (Lord Strathcona) 102
strikes 28, 50, 107, 132–33
  coal miners' strike of 1912–14 192, 211–12
suffrage (see votes for men, votes for women)

Taft, William 168, 174-75, 180
taxation 84, 214
temperance 23, 140, 205
Thompson, John 78, 81
Titanic 191
tobacco 218
Toronto 4, 141

trade 28, 80, 115, 135–36, 167, 189, 191
  free trade 5, 72, 83, 86, 88, 93, 134, 166, 176
  protectionism 32, 33, 36, 37, 44, 70, 71, 77, 85, 86, 88, 89, 93, 104–06, 118, 136, 165, 178–81, 195–96, 198, 215
  reciprocity 72, 80, 134, 172, 174–76, 178–83, 199
Tupper, Charles 15, 40, 68, 87, 97, 100, 103, 106, 112

unemployment 56, 212
unions 28, 50, 132–33, 170, 192
Upper Canada (see Ontario)
urbanization 44

Vancouver 153, 164, 216–17
Van Doos 223
Van Horne, William 93
veterans' pensions 31
votes for men 77
votes for women 53, 84, 96, 161–62, 185–86, 209

War of 1812 31
western alienation 89, 146, 148, 195–98, 215 (see also Riel Rebellion of 1885)
Whitney, James 188
Winnipeg 48, 137
Wolseley, Colonel Garnet 22
Women's Christian Temperance Union (WCTU) 114, 205
women's movement 25, 42, 54, 96, 133, 161–62, 207, 213 (see also votes for women)
World War I 219–25

Yukon 92, 97 (see also Alaska boundary dispute)